TREE MAGIC

The Path of Druids, Shamans, and Mystics

IVA KENAZ

Copyright © 2020 Iva Kenaz

First edition

All rights reserved. No part of this publication may be reproduced, stored in a retrieval system, or transmitted in any form or by any means, electronic, mechanical, photocopying, recording or otherwise without prior written permission from the author and publisher. For information visit *www.ivakenaz.com*

Author: Iva Kenaz

Illustrator: Ivana Axman

Editor: Jenny Papworth

Book and Cover Design: Iva Kenaz

ISBN: 9798675677290

CONTENTS

PART I
TREES IN MYTHOLOGY, MYSTICISM, AND SHAMANISM

1. World Tree of Life — 9
2. Axis Mundi: The Channel Between the Worlds — 27
3. Tree Deities, Elementals, and Human Tree Ancestors — 39
4. Tree Staff: The Conduit of Tree Magic — 55
5. Bird and Serpent: The Guardians of the Tree and Staff — 73
6. Trees, Cycles, and Us — 83

PART II
PRACTICAL TREE MAGIC

7. Our Tree of Life — 97
8. Tree Symbols, Signs, and Codes — 109
9. Working with Magic Staffs and Wands — 131
10. Tree Meditations, Journeying, and Rituals — 141

PART III
MAGIC OF INDIVIDUAL TREES

11. Druidic Goddess Trees — 157
12. Druidic God Trees — 169
13. Other Druidic Trees, Bushes, and Lianas — 177
14. Sacred Trees of Other Traditions — 193
Index — 206

ACKNOWLEDGEMENTS

A special thanks goes to my mom
Ivana Axman
who provided all the illustrations for this book
and who so lovingly supports me.
I would also like to thank Ayn Cates Sullivan,
Hana Sar Blochova, Eric Kaptein, and Vojta Jasny
for their unique wisdom and inspiration.

And finally, I send deep gratitude to my linden tree sisters
without whom this book would not come to be.

PART I

TREES IN MYTHOLOGY, MYSTICISM, AND SHAMANISM

This part of the book focuses on the World Tree of Life and our own Tree of Life.
It unveils the connection between trees, deities, animals, and humans, and delves into the divine potential of us all.

1

THE WORLD TREE OF LIFE

Trees are the source of life and some of the oldest living organisms on this planet. Although we no longer venerate them as our distant ancestors did, we are still aware that without them, we wouldn't be able to survive on this planet. Medicine and science teach us how trees affect our health and how well we thrive in their vicinity.

Throughout history, trees have been linked with various symbols, deities, and nature spirits, but the most unifying concepts of the ancient arts and mythologies are the Tree of Life and the World Tree. While the Tree of Life could be seen as the life force, the World Tree is the blueprint of our interdimensional reality. In unity, they are the World Tree of Life, the prototypal form that connects the micro to the macrocosm, and perhaps is the universe itself. The mystery of trees runs deep and their legacy stretches far, reflecting in the eternity above and below as well as the ever-changing flow of existence.

Trees represent the trinity of life, death, and rebirth in their cyclical story of a seed becoming a tree which gives life to new seeds. The trunk stands for the now and forever while the expansion of branches and roots demonstrates ceaseless growth, renewal, and therefore evolution. Together, this trinity epitomizes the interconnectedness of all life forms and their various expressions throughout the wheels of time. It's no wonder that trees have been found in mythology, legends, and art all over the world since the dawn of known history, as they reflect the "all within itself" and the "it within the all."

One of the oldest cultures we know of is the ancient Indian culture. The Indian Tree of Life is the Ashvattha Tree, sometimes described as the prototype of Brahman, the absolute reality, as well as a reflection of gods Brahma, Vishnu, and Shiva who embody the trinity of creation, preservation, and dissolution – in other words life, death, and rebirth or the past, present, and future. Just as in the Jewish Kabbalah, the Hindu Tree of Life is inverted. Sanskrit scriptures mention that the ancient scriptures, the Vedas, are its leaves, and that he who knows the Tree knows the Vedas and vice versa.

In Buddhism, the Ashvattha Tree is the Bodhi Tree, the Tree of Awakening under which Buddha reached enlightenment. In fact, Gautama Buddha was sometimes even depicted as a tree, and in the earliest Buddhistic texts, the tree was called the Awakener. Buddhistic legends say that beneath the Bodhi Tree is a diamond throne where all past Buddhas sat and achieved enlightenment.

During his inner spiritual adventures, Buddha learned that he needed to surpass the wheel of incarnation where the soul is trapped because of desire. Only once the spirit is detached from desire and finds the seat in the center of the wheel does it achieve true freedom. Then the spirit becomes the master of its being and not a pawn of someone else's mastery.

There's also a sacred wish-fulfilling tree in Hinduism and Buddhism called Kalpavriksha. Like many other Trees of Life or World Trees, it is located in a vast ocean or possibly celestial waters; this ocean is sometimes regarded as the birthplace of Sirius and compared to the Milky Way galaxy. At this tree resides a divine cow, Kamadhenu, which could be a counterpart to the Norse Auðhumbla, a celestial mother cow who licked the first giants out of the ice.

The Kalpavriksha Tree was believed to have golden roots, a silver trunk, branches of lapis lazuli, pearl flowers, and coral leaves, and its fruits were precious gems. The gems could be seen as stars or celestial bodies if we were to view it as the Cosmic Tree. In one myth, god Indra was believed to have planted the Kalpavriksha Tree in his kingdom. In another, the tree was originally located on earth but was misused by humans and so god Indra transferred it to his celestial paradise.

In ancient Sumer, the Tree of Life was described as growing from the center of the earth in the Garden of Edin, a name very similar to the biblical Garden of Eden. Its white, crystalline roots supposedly reached down into the primordial abyss and its branches carried the celestial spheres. The springs and streams beneath its soil nourished the land, and its foliage was home to all animal species, humans, spirits, and deities.

This sacred tree was viewed as a holy temple existing far beyond the mortal world. In the tree's heart lived god Enki (known as Ea in Babylonian and Akkadian). He was the god of wisdom and earth, and the creator of mankind. At night he descended into the holy waters beneath the tree and at sunrise he rose to its branches, following the daily cycle of the sun. The connection between the tree and the sun is extensive and will be discussed in more detail in the following chapters.

Since the sun and Tree of Life symbolism have been linked throughout ancient history, it's quite plausible that Enki was a sun god as well as a tree god. In this regard, it's also worth mentioning that Enki's son Asari shared some attributes with the Egyptian god Osiris who was also a sun and tree god and whose name meant "the seat of the eye."

In the *Epic of Gilgamesh*, the Tree of Life, or the Cosmic Tree, is introduced as an eternal form encompassing the whole universe and existing far beyond the gates of the vast waters. Since the sky was often referred to as the celestial waters in ancient times, the vastness of these waters could be even broader. In the epic, Gilgamesh enters an enchanted forest where the trees of gods grow and thrive. Like the Indian Kalpavriksha Tree, these divine trees bear precious gems instead of common fruits, which in a cosmic sense may represent stars. They also shoot crystals from the soil and provide shade to marvelous birds whose nests are also made of precious stones.

The ancient Assyrian Tree of Life was usually depicted between two mythical animal figures such as griffins, cherubs, or unicorns. A curious winged disk is often seen above it, which could represent the supreme gods or the sun.

In ancient Egypt, the Tree of Life, or more likely the Cosmic Tree, was seen as a holy sycamore (fig) with the sun god Osiris living in its branches. Osiris was also called "one with the tree" and the ancient Egyptians believed that after his death, a tree grew around his body and enclosed it in its trunk. The tree was later cut down and made into a pillar, which goddess Isis retrieved in order to extract Osiris's body from it. After that, the pillar was called the *djed* and symbolized Osiris's spine. The relation between spine and tree will be mentioned again as it's crucial in Hindu yoga practice and the kundalini awakening.

God Osiris was a deity of light and love who guided souls on their path into the other realms of the World Tree. That's why his tomb was depicted as both a tree and a gateway.

The Phoenicians, whose name means both "phoenix" and "date palm," had their own Tree of Life. It was an ethereal olive tree that grew from two rocks floating in the sea (or the celestial waters). An eagle perched on its crown and a dragon lived in its branches.

What is most curious about this tree, however, is that it was believed to thrive on fire, which didn't harm the wood and actually made its branches shine like a candelabra. This mirrors the related sun and tree symbolism in Mesopotamia and Egypt. It also bears a similarity to the biblical story of Moses and the burning bush, because in that story the fire didn't hurt the bush either and actually contained a powerful message, as God spoke to Moses through the fire, encouraging him to free his people.

Another strange fiery light phenomenon has been witnessed in the sacred Grove of Mamre where the biblical prophet Abraham lived and encountered God, and where he was later buried. Witnesses described that although one of the trees seemed to be on fire, it remained unharmed by the flames. They considered it the haunt of angels and therefore regularly presented the tree with cakes, wine, and myrrh to pay their respects to the celestial guardians.

The legend of the burning tree or the Tree of Light has been preserved to this day in the symbolism of the menorah, the sacred Jewish candelabra. It is even more fascinating that a seven-headed being that actually resembles the candelabra has been found among various petroglyphs all over the world, usually portrayed next to a tree and a Sun Wheel, which is one of the most crucial Tree of Life symbols.

The Tree of Light can be seen in the Rider Waite version of the Tarot where it stands beside the male figure in the Lovers trump. This connection is significant as the Tarot cards are supposed to contain all the teachings and symbolism of the Torah, the Kabbalistic book of prayers that actually translates as "instruction" or "teaching." The menorah has seven branches and is seen as a representation of the seven classical planets with the sun at its center. In ancient cultures, the seven planets were viewed as the seven heavens or celestial spheres. Interestingly, Islamic paradise is a garden situated in the seventh heaven and at its center stands a tree called Tooba.

Sun Wheel and Tree of Life
as depicted by Balkan Celts
(inspired by Celtic Thasos tetradrachms).

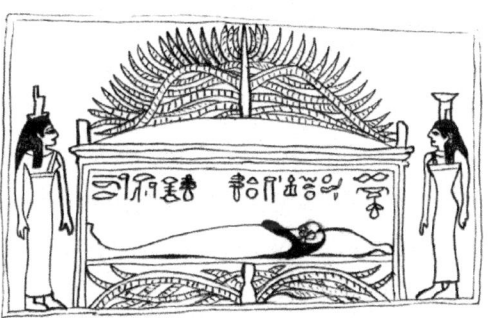
Osiris entombed in a tree
(inspired by ancient Egyptian art).

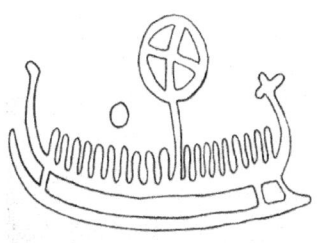
Sun Wheel and ship into
another world (ships of renewal)
from Bronze Age Sweden.

Mesopotamian Tree of Life
(inspired by the cylinder seal).

The seven-headed figure resembling the Jewish menorah. In this picture,
inspired by Siberian cave paintings from 5000 BC, it stands beside a spiked wheel and a tree.
Notice that on the left, there are clear runic inscriptions.

In ancient Persia, there was the Gaokerena Tree meaning "ox horn." However, it was also called the Haoma Tree after the spirit who animated it. The tree was considered the source of life: a unifier and nourisher all of creation. It grew from the mud beneath the wide ocean bed, which could be symbolic for the celestial waters. The Haoma Tree bears stars as fruit, which could link to the precious gems produced by the Sumerian and Indian World Trees. It's also the tree whose spirit guides souls into the afterlife.

As in many other legends and mythologies, the tree has a reptilian enemy as well as an ally. The Persian Tree of Life had a wicked lizard that had to be tamed by ten serpent-like fish guardians. Thanks to them, the tree remained unharmed and expanded into eternity. Throughout history and mythology, serpents have belonged to tree symbolism, and though some are wise guides, others pose as devious tricksters.

In the Bible, we learn about Adam and Eve and the two trees that, as many scholars pointed out, could actually be one and the same: the Tree of Knowledge of Good and Evil and the Tree of Life. Here, the tree is a symbol of temptation and sin, which was orchestrated by a serpentine being. Tree symbolism also connects to Jesus Christ. The Tree of Jesse or the Jesse Tree was depicted in various Christian artworks as the family tree of Jesus's ancestors, and this inspired the family-tree charts we still use today.

There's also the legend of the Nehushtan, a holy pole with a bronze or copper serpent that Moses built to protect the Israelites from attack by the fiery sky serpents. Early Christians, Jews, and Muslims commonly held meetings in sacred tree groves, and trees – or their symbolic representatives, the staffs or rods – became attributes of many saints and patriarchs. In ancient Israel, poles and pillars representing the Cosmic Tree were erected in sacred locations dedicated to goddess Asherah, the nature goddess of fertility and growth.

The Jewish Tree of Life was preserved in the Torah. The Kabbalists see the tree as a blueprint of God's creation of the world and the spiritual journey that humans undergo on their way to enlightenment. The tree is believed to have three basic spheres that epitomize the main principles of the universe. This basic trinity reoccurs in many philosophies and religions as life, death, and rebirth; past, present, and future; or light, dark, and shadow.

The Jewish Tree of Life was an almond tree, whose ancient name is *luz*, a word that represents the nut as well as the tree itself. Curiously, luz translates as "light" in Old Portuguese and therefore takes us back to sun/tree symbolism. The word "luz" was also associated with the luz bone, which is believed to be the first cervical vertebra, the atlas bone, that supports the head on the spine. *The Zohar*, the literary foundation of Kabbalistic teachings, compares this bone to the head of a serpent. Kabbalistic mysticism regards this bone as the indestructible seed from which the body can be resurrected. Interestingly, an injury to the atlas bone is sometimes a cause of Alzheimer's disease. We could therefore view the luz or atlas bone as the memory disk of the human body.

The Kabbalistic Tree of Life was depicted upside down, and some mystics consider this to be only half the riddle. If we apply the hermetic principle "as above, so below" and merge the Kabbalistic Tree of Life with its mirror image, the result is two hexagrams, two Stars of David, or perhaps two coalesced worlds.

Ancient Mesopotamian gods (possibly Enki and Enlil) by the Tree of Life (inspired by ancient Mesopotamian art).

Couples by the Tree of Life (inspired by the Phoenician scarab corpus).

The old Germanic and Norse tribes had a World Tree called Yggdrasil, a multidimensional complex of three basic spheres – the primordial, cosmic, and terrestrial – which further divided into nine different realms: the realms of men, dwarfs, dark elves, giants, bright elves, original Germanic deities called Vanir, Aesir gods, and the archetypal realms of the two basic elements of ice and fire. The realms of dwarves and dark elves were later merged into one and a realm called Hel was added as the place where souls depart to if they don't die in battle.

The three main roots of the Yggdrasil grew from two sacred wells and one hot spring. One of the wells belonged to the god of ancestral memory, Mímir, and the other was occupied by two swans and a trinity of female giants called Norns. The Norns carved the sacred runic alphabet into the tree and set the destiny of men. The spring was considered the source of all waters and the home of the serpentine beings.

Like the ancient Indian and Mesopotamian World Trees, the Yggdrasil also had sacred birds living in its branches and serpents guarding the trunk and roots. One of them was a mighty serpent called Jormungadr who guarded the river of ocean or, in a cosmic sense, the celestial ocean, perhaps symbolic for the Dark Rift at the center of the Milky Way.

The other one, Níðhöggr, was regarded sometimes as a serpent and at other times as a worm or a dragon who lived in the roots and gnawed at them, though it never succeeded in destroying them. A squirrel called Ratatoskr traveled between the roots and the crown and carried messages between Níðhöggr, an eagle, and a hawk that sat between the eagle's eyes, probably representing his third eye.

The Germanic tribe of Saxons had their own depiction of the Tree of Life: the great pillar Irminsul made from a tree trunk and worshiped as a connection between the heavenly and earthly realms. The older name for Irminsul was Jörmunr, which was also one of the sacred names of god Odin. However, there was also a Germanic god called Irmin that the Irminsul related to.

In the legends of the ancient Baltic cultures, the World Tree was sometimes called the Sun Tree as it was associated with the yearly solar cycles. Like many other Trees of Life, it was located in the midst of an ocean, which could represent the celestial waters if viewed as the Cosmic Tree.

There is not much known about the Slavic tribes because of a lack of literary sources, but some information has been gained from excavations. We have discovered that tree groves were common sanctums for these people as sacred objects containing symbolism were found there. The most common was the Sun Wheel or the wheel of the year, which may stand for the Sun Tree. Interestingly, like the Germanic and Norse tribes, the Slavs regarded the sun as having a female quality, which contradicts later medieval European mysticism where the moon represented the female and the sun had male qualities.

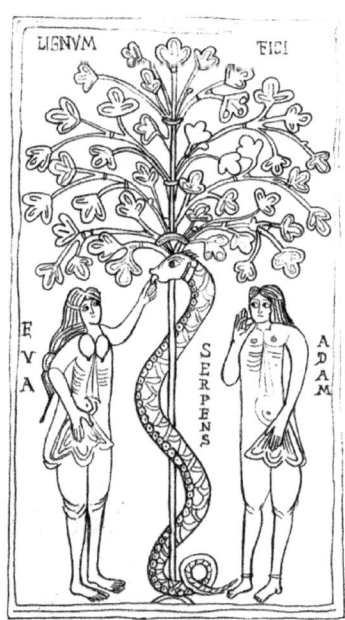

Adam and Eve
(inspired by the 10th-century Codex Vigilanus).

Uralian Tree of Life
(inspired by ancient Mesopotamian art).

World Pillar as depicted
on an ancient Greek coin.

The Finno-Ugric peoples of Northeast Europe and North Asia had a world pillar, a pole that kept the order of the universe in place. It was also perceived as a ladder that the souls of the departed could climb to reach the celestial realms. Similarly, the biblical Jacob's Ladder was a celestial ladder used by angels to ascend into the heavenly realms or descend to earth as described by the patriarch Jacob.

The Sámi or the Lapps, the indigenous Finno-Urgic peoples, still depict the Tree of Life on their shamanic drums, sometimes in the shape of crosses or spiked wheels. These symbols are often accompanied by U shapes and M shapes that were found abundantly on Bronze Age artifacts. The U shapes probably represented the entrances to the other worlds as they resemble gateways or earth crevices. As for the M shapes and zigzags, these could stand for the waters, possibly celestial ones, that the spirit crossed over before reaching the spirit realms.

The indigenous peoples of the Baikal region in Siberia – the Buryats and Tunguses – revere trees and regard them as mediators between the celestial and earthly spheres. They have a special respect for trees with strong trunks, which they call mother trees. They also believe that if a large number of trees are cut down, many people will die. Women in labor traditionally hold on to a rod or staff to transfer the pain into the ground. The local shamans also achieve healing while sitting, meditating, or dozing off under trees. To show their high regard for trees, they decorate tree trunks with ribbons, especially gold and silver ones, the colors of the sun and moon.

The Buryats have a special connection to the birch and consider it to be of divine origin because it represents their original mother, the sacred white swan. Even to this day, the Buryat shamans climb birches to attune to the celestial mother swan and erect ritual poles in honor of the Cosmic Tree, which are then decorated with colorful ribbons. The mother swan could be linked to the Swan constellation located at the center of our galaxy, but more on that in chapter two.

As in Siberia, trees were also decorated in ancient Greece, particularly with ribbons, garlands, or flutes which were usually gifts to the god of wildlife Pan, who was called Faunus in ancient Rome. We don't find a Tree of Life as such in this Mediterranean culture because the mythology revolves more around the sun, but as we know, the tree and the sun have always been interlinked.

There's a curious Greek legend about the sacred apple tree in Hera's orchard. The tree bore golden apples that clearly recall the precious fruits and gems growing on the Sumerian and Hindu Trees of Life. This tree had its soil in the Garden of the Hesperides, named after the nymphs who guarded it by dancing around it and singing all day until the Hesperus (Venus) rose in the sky. An additional guardian of the tree was the hundred-headed dragon called Ladon. Here, we meet another serpentine creature at a sacred tree, and although it is a guardian rather than a monster, it ends up being slaughtered by Heracles who stole the golden apples.

In Celtic mythology, we find sacred apple orchards similar to the Greek Garden of the Hesperides, and one legend even coincides quite literally. It's the one about the sun god Llew or Lugh who asked the sons of Tuireann to acquire three apples from the Garden of the Hesperides. The apples were described as magical fruits that granted wishes. They had a honey-like taste, were burnished gold in color, and grew much bigger than common apples. All diseases were cured and all wounds healed when they were consumed and, miraculously, they didn't diminish after being eaten.

The legend of the Isle of the Blessed also called the Elysian Fields unites Celtic and Greek mythology as both are described as a heavenly paradise where heroes lived in a mild climate, surrounded by sweet fruit trees and wondrous birds. The Isle of the Blessed was located in the River Oceanus, and some believe this was or perhaps still is located in the mysterious Bermuda triangle. The isle was a special place for souls who chose to incarnate into this world only three times and managed to preserve their spirit in purity.

Yet another sacred apple orchard was the Affalenau where Merlin went to rejuvenate and receive wisdom. Its apples could be digested only by some, and the trees held the wisdom of the earth, its cycles, and planetary movements. For all we know, it could have been an orchard in an ethereal plane of existence or in Merlin's inner world.

The Celtic Tree of Life has been depicted as a tree with its branches and roots entwined, symbolizing the interconnectedness of the roots, trunk, and branches; the past, present, and future; and the netherworld, earth, and heaven. To the Celts, trees were gateways into the otherworldly realms. Tree spirits, who were able to travel in between these worlds, were considered wise teachers and guides. The Irish and Welsh words for trees, *fid* and *gwydd*, relate to the words *fios* and *gywddon* that translate as "wisdom." Like many ancient tribes, the Celts also revered trees, and it was strictly forbidden to fell sacred trees as they often housed powerful beings, even ancestors. Celtic tree magic is mainly affiliated with the ogham, the sacred tree alphabet that will be discussed in chapter eight.

The Druids were powerful in Celtic society as they were considered mediators between the worlds of the gods and men. They were believed to follow similar teachings as the Pythagoreans because they also studied the science of nature, astronomy, math, and physiology. As apparent from the legends they shared, they have probably influenced each other and perhaps even shared the same source. After all, Greek and Celtic cultures merged in continental Europe before the Celtic tribes moved to the British Isles.

Since the ogham Duir means "oak," Druids have also been mainly associated with the oak tree. However, there are more tree correlations in the name: Old Irish *druï* or *druí* means "diviner" or "wizard," and in Proto-Celtic, *dru-wid* translates as "tree-knower." The Sanskrit word *dru* means "tree" or "wood," and in Old English, the word *duru* means "door" or "gate." This fortifies the shamanic concept of trees acting as gateways into the other worlds. It could also elucidate why the ancient Paleolithic, Egyptian, Sumerian, and Jewish Trees of Life were depicted next to a gate or an entrance of some kind.

Like many ancient cultures, the indigenous peoples of North, Central, and South America saw trees as thresholds into otherworldly dimensions. Local shamans or medicine men journeyed through trees to receive guidance, wisdom, and healing. They descended or ascended into trees depending on which realm they wished to visit.

The Mayan Tree of Life or World Tree was the sacred ceiba called *wacah chan* or *ya'axche*, meaning "the first tree." It was seen as a giant tree holding the world together. As in many other mythologies, there were three main spheres within it: the inner, the outer, and the central one. The crown was often depicted as four branches that symbolized the four cardinal directions. As in other parts of the world, the Mayan Tree of Life was depicted as a cross where the middle epitomized the center of the universe. This tree should be viewed as the Cosmic Tree since it's mainly regarded as a symbolic interpretation of our galaxy.

The descendants of the Incas, the Q'ero who live in Cusco, Peru, also divide the cosmos into three spheres: the celestial world, the netherworld, and the terrestrial world that we experience. The Lakota and almost all Plains Indian tribes held sacred the Sun Tree, which was represented at ceremonies in the form of an erected pole. During each yearly sun dance, the community fasted and gave offerings when they gathered at the pole. Sometimes, young warriors pierced their skin with a bone and attached it to the thongs that hung from the pole. Then they would dance around the pole to transcend their pain and reach higher states of consciousness. Native American totem poles were also carved from tree trunks and represented the spirit of the land.

26

2

Axis Mundi:

The Channel Between the Worlds

The axis mundi is the central line between the celestial poles, the World Pillar, but also the tunnel or tree trunk through which shamans journey into other realms. The word *šaman* (shaman) comes from Siberian Tungusic languages and means "the one who knows" because a shaman is well aware that this reality is just a tiny branch of an ever-growing World Tree, Tree of Life, or simply World Tree of Life.

Ever since ancient times, trees – especially hollow ones – have been known to hide secret entrances into otherworldly dimensions. Shamans describe the journey through the axis mundi as traveling through a channel or climbing a tree, a pole, or a ladder that takes their light body into the other dimensions while their physical body grounds them in local time and space. Shamans ascend or descend the axis mundi depending on their intention, and which place they resonate with at a given moment. The branches usually lead to the future or the celestial realms while the roots meander into the past or the inner earth realms. The axis mundi is the trunk of the tree, the central pole that connects the above and below and the within and without. Shamans journey into the other realms mainly to receive healing, wisdom, and guidance on their spiritual path.

The portals may be not only in trees but also in the ground, caves, wells, or springs; however, these are usually located next to sacred trees. In his book, *The Way of the Shaman*, author Michael Harner mentions that when the Conibo Indians journey, they follow the roots of a giant catahua tree. The roots eventually turn into serpents that guide them through a myriad of realities.

Serpents accompany the World Tree of Life in many mythologies, along with birds, winged creatures, and various primordial deities; more on that in the following chapters. Serpents were seen as magical animals, the guardians of life and wisdom. They were powerful allies, guides, and protectors of humans on the path to enlightenment. Many mystics believe that they are also symbolic of spiraling energy, which represents the creative powers of nature as well as our spiritual force that is waiting to be awakened: the kundalini.

Although our modern societies now tend to be out of balance and not as strongly bound to trees and forests as they were in the times of our distant ancestors, the World Tree of Life is still alive and vibrant. In many ways, we could compare the World Tree of Life to the electromagnetic field that protects and preserves the planet and all the living organisms on it.

This electromagnetic field arises from the center and creates a flow of opposing yet unifying forces that result in a living energy field. Therefore, the flow from above connects to the flow from below through the within in the central vortex and embraces the whole. We could say that it encapsulates the hermetic "as above, so below" or "as within, so without."

The field has a toroidal shape, and the torus is the most harmonious geometric shape with a perpetual self-sustaining, self-organizing, self-renewing, ever-flowing quality. The torus could be seen as the World Tree of Life where the vortex is the trunk and the constant flow of two opposing energies creates the unity of the branches and roots. It may not be a coincidence that the Celtic Tree of Life, where the branches and roots entwine, bears a resemblance to the torus (see chart).

The physicist and expert on electromagnetic fields, James Clerk Maxwell, considered the fifth element – the ether – to be the transmission medium for the electromagnetic field. We could therefore say that the electromagnetic field of the planet, or its life source, is a reflection of this most mysterious element that encompasses and permeates the other basic elements.

The electromagnetic field of humans and animals emanates from the heart and follows the same self-organizing energy flux as that of the planet. It's probably also the source of a self-revitalizing, self-sustaining ability we all inherently have. I like to call this field our Tree of Life so I will refer to it as such henceforth. Our Tree of Life and the electromagnetic field is the key to understanding our life force and our light body, also known as the Merkaba, which allows us to shift between dimensions in the World Tree of Life.

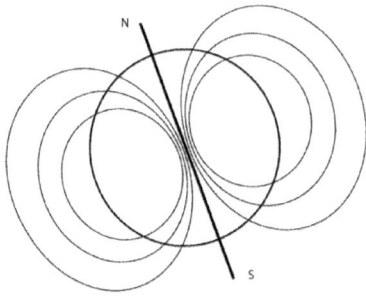

The electromagnetic field of the Earth.

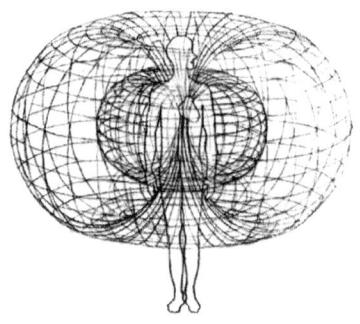

The electromagnetic field of the heart.

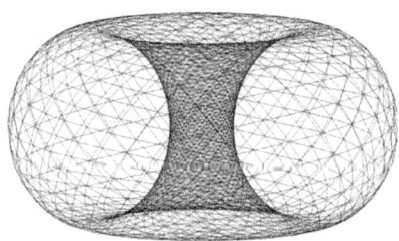

Torus

The Celtic Tree of Life and the torus.

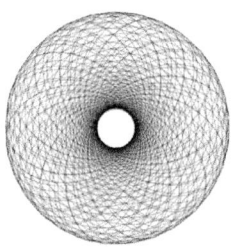

The torus from above swirls in concentric circles.

The spiraling motion of the vortex in the electromagnetic field.

But back now to the axis mundi. In a philosophical sense, the axis mundi is the central trunk of the World Tree of Life and the channel between its multidimensional realms and timelines. In a cosmic sense, the axis mundi is the central pole of the earth and, together with its electromagnetic field, it resembles a torus. In a geometric sense, it's the central vortex of the torus, a whirling and spiraling double cone, which also resembles the figure-of-eight symbol of eternity (see chart).

When shamans pass through the axis mundi, they often find themselves surrounded by a stream of light. Sometimes this stream has two directions, one leading to the north and the other to the south, which clearly links to the vortex of the earth's electromagnetic field that connects the South and North Poles.

It can't be a coincidence that people who have had an out-of-body experience describe their crossing into the afterlife as a journey through a tunnel of light. Could it be that the vortex of the electromagnetic field of the earth is, at a different level of existence, the channel that connects the earthly dimension with the more ethereal ones? This tunnel could also be the great pillar of the Finno-Urgic peoples or the Irminsul of the Saxons that were also channels between the heavenly and earthly realms. In Christian mysticism, this was the ladder or stairway to heaven, which bears a striking similarity to how shamans describe their journeying into the otherworldly realms.

Other sacred channels that lead into the afterlife have been described as rivers, streams, or bridges; perhaps for that reason, trees were often depicted on boats. In the Norse World Tree, the connection between the earthly and ethereal spheres is the rainbow bridge called Bifröst. A similar interdimensional bridge, sometimes regarded as a ladder, appears in Irish and Scottish legends as well.

It was either called the Drochet Bethad – the Bridge of Life – or the Drochaid na Flaitheanas – the Bridge of Heaven.

The shamanic entrance into the interdimensional channel of the axis mundi is described as a whirl of concentric circles, suggesting that it could be the vortex of the electromagnetic field. But there's an interesting connection to trees here. When a living tree is cut diagonally in half, we notice concentric circles that grow around the original sapling. This sapling becomes the strongest part of the tree: its spine, so to speak. The last ring of the trunk, which is just below the bark is the cambium layer, the most vital layer responsible for new growth and regeneration. That's why when foresters "ring" trees they condemn them to a slow death as the tree can't feed itself anymore. Logging and felling for profit, and all the unnecessary interference with bioprocesses in woodlands, show us how far people have distanced themselves from nature and trees. As Vojtěch Jasný, a visionary Czech filmmaker and mystic, once said: "It's possible to lose the Tree of Life. A felled tree is a stereotype of destruction – cutting down a sapling in its growth…"

In some trees, the original sapling decays and the tree becomes hollow, similar to the torus, the geometric shape of the electromagnetic field. Yew is one of these trees, and since it's a long-living and constantly regenerating tree, it demonstrates just how powerful the hollowed toroidal energy is. Maybe for this reason, the yew has been regarded as the World Tree in Germanic and Norse mythologies.

The Tibetan mandalas, which inspire deep meditation or trance, also consist of concentric circles. These mandalas can be seen as two-dimensional depictions of a torus. Concentric circles and their derived shapes such as spirals can be found in many shamanic artworks and are often depicted on ceremonial drums used during interdimensional journeying. The Alaskan shamans even wear masks with concentric circles that arise from a central void.

The electromagnetic field and its geometric depiction, the torus, follow a circular, spiraling motion during which energy flows from and returns to the center. In a two-dimensional form, this would be best depicted as concentric circles or spirals. The vortex of the torus, however, could be compared to a sand clock, a figure of eight, or a spindle, which links to the three archetypal females, the Norns, Fates, or Sudicky, who spin the destiny of the World Tree of Life. All these geometric shapes and symbols are known as representing eternity, which also pertains to the flow of the electromagnetic field.

A curious connection can be found in the "Myth of Er" from Plato's *Republic*. In the story, the hero, Er, sees the souls of the dead traveling through a channel of rainbow-colored light, which is described as "the great spindle of eight concentric spheres rotating under the supervision of sirens and three Fates," the daughters of the goddess Necessity. It is by this celestial spindle that the souls decide where to incarnate next. Er even witnesses how some humans choose to be born as animals and vice versa. Each soul is also provided with a guardian for that specific lifetime and then passes over to the realms of oblivion and forgetfulness before proceeding to the new incarnation. Although most history books don't mention the ancient Greeks' belief in reincarnation, this legend states it quite clearly.

This curious celestial spindle of eight spheres could be the interdimensional channel or the vortex of the earth's electromagnetic field. After all, in the Norse World Tree, eight different worlds can be reached from the ninth one where humans live...

Besides trees, shamans journey into the other worlds through holes in the earth. The Bella Coola Indians even had a hole in the ground of their homes that functioned as an interdimensional threshold. Such portals could also hide in sacred wells and springs, or under large stones. As in the case of tree portals, the exit is not always at the same location as the entrance, and shamans have to be prepared for this in order to find their way back. The earthly entrances could be a part of the system of ley lines that connect various sacred sites all over the globe and create a large grid or net of the earth's energy field.

Hallowed entrances into the netherworlds, or the inner earth as it's sometimes called, were also known to Irish and Icelandic cultures. They were inhabited by the Sidhe, also known as the "hidden people," who are sometimes considered to be identical to the elves.

In Celtic and Norse mythologies, sacred springs and wells have an important place in the World Tree. They are at the tree's base, by the roots, and sometimes they are considered a reflection of the archetypal, divine mind. The well of Mímir, through which god Odin reached enlightenment after he hung himself upside down on the mighty Yggdrasil, translates as the "well of ancestral memory."

Odin legendarily threw one of his eyes into the well, and although most scholars conclude that it was one of his physical eyes, it could have been his third eye. After all, our third eye is the pineal gland, which has a liquid inside it and could therefore be perceived as a symbolic well.

Irminsul,
the old Saxon pillar of heaven.

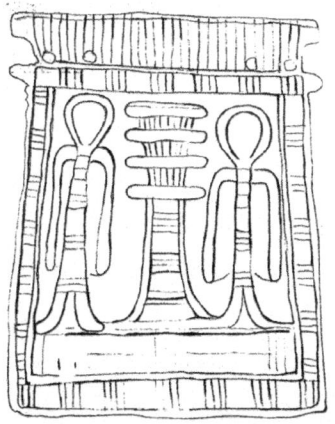

Ancient Egyptian djed pillar
in between two beings
that resemble the ankh cross.

The ladder to heaven
as depicted in the Morgan Bible,
13th-century France.

Axis mundi as the tree (below)
and serpent (above) in a boat.
(These Swedish Bronze Age
ships are regarded as ships of renewal.)

In Celtic mythology, sacred springs and wells are guarded by goddesses such as Brigid, Sirona, or Coventina, who imbue the waters with gifts of intuition and psychic powers including the ability to experience the otherworldly realms. In Norse mythology, three giantesses called Norns guard the Urðarbrunnr, the well of fate next to which they spin the destiny of the world. And at that well suffused with milky white water lives a pair of swans. In mythology and legend, swans pertain to holy springs, trees, and shrines. Through his profound research and publications, author Andrew Collins proved that many ancient sites such as Avebury in England, the pyramids of Giza, or the mysterious Gobekli Tepe in Turkey were built to reflect the celestial star constellation of the Cygnus, which is Latin for "swan."

The Swan constellation lies at the Great Rift, also known as the Dark River, which conceals the center of the Milky Way galaxy from the earth's perspective. We could therefore say that it lies beside the axis mundi of our galaxy's electromagnetic field. Even though the electromagnetic fields of galaxies are weaker, they run on the same principle as that of the celestial bodies. Perhaps that's why many ancient cultures saw the Swan constellation as a sky portal. If the planetary axis takes us into the other dimensions of the earth, could the axis mundi of the Milky Way lead us into other dimensions of the galaxy?

Interestingly, the World Tree of Life is often described as having sacred bird and serpent guardians, and what accompanies the Swan constellation in the sky? The Eagle constellation Aquila and the Serpent constellation Serpen. Moreover, galaxies have been called cosmic serpents due to their spiraling shape.

The swan is a water bird, and in a symbolic sense it occupies the earthly and celestial waters. That's why so many sky deities were depicted as riding swans or ducks. Moreover, the Swan constellation not only bears a similarity to a descending swan from the earth's point of view, but it also resembles a few symbols and runes that have represented trees and the World Tree of Life in the ancient past. These are crosses, rune Algiz which actually translates as "swan," and rune Tiwaz that symbolizes the World Pillar or Irminsul.

It's intriguing that the ancients considered the Swan constellation to be the place of origin, and the Siberian Baikal tribes still believe that they descended from a birch tree and the heavenly mother swan. There's definitely some greater mystery surrounding this star constellation and the Dark Rift near the center of our galaxy.

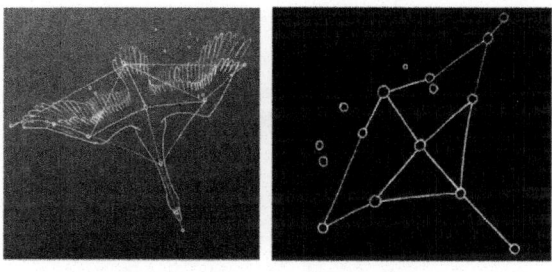

The Cygnus (Swan) star constellation.

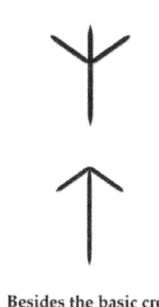

Besides the basic cross,
the Cygnus constellation
conceals rune Algiz (above)
and Tiwaz (below).

Many deities roamed
the heavens on swans.
Here is the Greek goddess
Aphrodite on her swan
(based on an ancient Greek fresco).

38

3

Tree Deities, Elementals, and Human Tree Ancestors

The attribution of divine spirits to trees was natural to most ancient cultures. In the ancient Hindu text *Puranas*, we learn that the father of humankind, Daksha, was actually the son of Marisha, the daughter of trees who married the lord Pracheta to appease him when he decided to cut down the overgrown forests.

Brahman, the supreme Hindu deity, is a tree that bears the other gods and goddesses in its branches. Brahman is also seen as the omnipresent divine presence encompassing "the all." The most acclaimed Buddha, Siddhartha, had forty-three previous tree incarnations and reached his enlightenment under the Bodhi Tree. Before he became one with the tree, however, he underwent many tests. First, the chief of demons tried to break him with terrifying apparitions and by throwing fire, rocks, and even mountains at him, but Siddhartha managed to change the rocks to flowers and the fire to rainbow light. He remained calm even while being tempted by beautiful women. His enlightenment was likened to being centered in the wheel of creation, as only in the center can one remain unattached and free.

In many other tree and enlightenment stories, a wise serpent becomes a guardian to the initiate, and for Buddha it was Mucalinda, the king of the Nagi, who were benevolent half-serpent, half-human beings. Mucalinda protected him from the harshness of the heavy rain that fell upon him during the seven days of darkness he had to withstand.

Trees were also home to various Egyptian deities and nature devas who sometimes emerged in human form to provide guidance to mortals. The roots of such spirited trees were nourished by the River Nile and the locals kept jars of water by their trunks as offerings or brought other gifts such as fruits and vegetables. The tree devas were believed to enjoy poetry, and people often recited poems to them or sang ballads.

The sycamore tree was regarded as an earthly incarnation of the sky goddesses Hathor and Nuit. Hathor's spirit was actually believed to animate sycamores, and that's why she was also called the "goddess of the sacred tree." As in many other ancient cultures, trees were seen as thresholds to the otherworldly realms. That's why these holy trees guarded the gates to the netherworld and the land of the dead.

The Persea Tree gave the knowledge of writing and was often

depicted with the deities of language, Thoth and Seshat, writing on its trunk or branches. Interestingly, Thoth connects the World Tree of Life's tree, bird, and serpent symbolism as he was most commonly depicted with the head of an ibis, holding serpents, and standing by trees.

The Phoenicians believed that their progenitors venerated trees as gods and thus gave them precious offerings. The ancient culture of Canaan built tree altars and tree-like posts and decorated them with ribbons as did the indigenous people of the Baikal. For all the ancients, trees were considered oracles and wise teachers.

In ancient Mesopotamia, the Tree of Life was the home of god Enki (also known as Ea in Akkadian and Babylonian cultures). He was the god of wisdom, the lord of the earth, and the creator of mankind who lived in the heart of the tree. The goddess Inanna (later known as Ishtar) was also commonly depicted standing beside a tree or in tree form.

In the "Myth of Inanna, Gilgamesh, and the Huluppu Tree," Inanna plants a huluppu (willow) tree in the Garden of Edin. She plans on making her throne from the tree's wood, but then one of the *lilu* (meaning spirits of the wild) called Lilith inhabits it along with her serpent and a lion-headed bird. Inanna asks the hero, Gilgamesh, to cut the tree down and banish the bird, serpent, and Lilith. Though Gilgamesh's father was also one of the lilu, in this story we see him defeating one of his own kind. Willow seems to be an important tree in Mesopotamian mythology as the Sumerian

Belili, the goddess of the moon and love, was believed to animate willow trees, sacred wells, and springs.

Sometimes, there were half-human, half-serpent deities linked with the Tree of Life as well. For example, the Mesopotamian Ningishzida, the god of the World Tree of Life, was depicted as a serpent or represented by a symbol strikingly similar to the staff of Greek god Hermes, the caduceus (see chart). He was also a god of nature, healing, fertility, and the netherworld.

Like trees, serpents are also considered our progenitors or ancestors in many mythologies. For example, Fuxi and Nuwa were the Chinese serpentine deities with human heads who created human beings out of clay. Fuxi is also known as the creator of the *I Ching* and Nuwa as the repairer of the pillars of heaven.

The Babylonian Chaldeans had a sacred cedar tree of god Ea, and this tree was believed to restore health and act as the channel between the heavens and earth. As in many other ancient cultures, trees were oracles in Mesopotamia. The *Epic of Izdubar* mentions a sacred tree that listens and speaks.

In ancient Persia, there's a legend about the spiritual leader Zoroaster encountering Haoma, the World Tree of Life deity, who gave vitality to bodies and provided enlightenment to souls. He is also described as the way to heaven – the one who guides souls into eternal life.

Zoroaster himself was also affiliated with a tree and was actually believed to have turned into a tall tree upon his death. His teachings also mention that the first human couple, Machina and Maschiana, developed from a tree in the Garden of Heden, which clearly refers to the Mesopotamian Edin and biblical Eden.

The most ancient religion of all, Zoroastrianism (the religion of Zoroaster), revered trees, especially the cypress tree, which was linked to the benevolent god Ormuzd and the sun god Mithra, and worshiped with the sacred fire pertaining to tree symbolism.

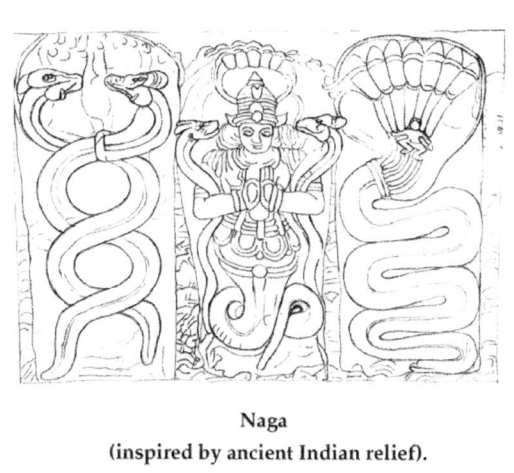

Naga
(inspired by ancient Indian relief).

A man with serpents
(drawing inspired by the
Celtic Tully Lough Cross
from the 8th to 9th century).

Sumerian god Ningizidda
(inspired by ancient Sumerian art).

Caduceus

Woman with two serpents
(possibly goddess Frigga),
inspired by a 5th-century stone relief
in Gotland, Sweden.

Ancient Mesopotamian
or Egyptian caduceus.

Minoan priestess holding
two serpents.

The Semite peoples had earth and nature deities called *baal* that translates as "spirits of vegetation." Many heroes and deities were baals; for example, Heracles was called the Baal of Tyre and goddess Astarte, the Baal of Babylon, because the true names of the deities were often hidden from common people so as not to be misused.

In ancient Greece, various deities were affiliated with sacred trees. Oak was the tree of the main god of Olympus, Zeus, and his spirit was believed to animate the sacred oak at the Dodona oracle. His wife, goddess Hera, was born beneath a willow, but another one of her beloved trees was pear. The sun god Apollo was brought into the world under a date palm but was also affiliated with laurel and apple as some historians assume that the word "apple" derives from his original name, Apellon.

The main attributes of goddess Athena were the olive tree, the serpent, and the owl, which unite the familiar tree–serpent–bird symbolism of the World Tree of Life. Another god whose attributes combine this archetypal trinity was Hermes, the god of the wilderness, whose tree staff, the caduceus, had two serpents coiled around it and bird wings atop. His symbol was also the *herm*, a pillar with a human head on the top and a protruding phallus. The herm also decorated roadsides as Hermes was a god of trade and communication. He was also a powerful psychopomp and led souls into the afterlife with his magic staff, which symbolically represented the World Tree of Life.

The goddess of love, Aphrodite, was associated with an apple tree and myrrh because her lover, Adonis, was born from a myrrh tree. The goddess of the wild and of the yearly and moon cycles, Artemis (Roman Diana) was not linked to any specific tree species, but she was known to roam Greek woodlands. Artemis also had a bear cult, which could make her a counterpart of the Finnish goddess of woods and wild animals, Mielikki, who was believed to have created the bear species and was an esteemed animal healer and herbalist.

Mother Earth
(inspired by an 11th-century
Italian parchment illustration).

Ancient Greek coin depicting
goddess Athena and her attributes
pertaining to the World Tree of Life.

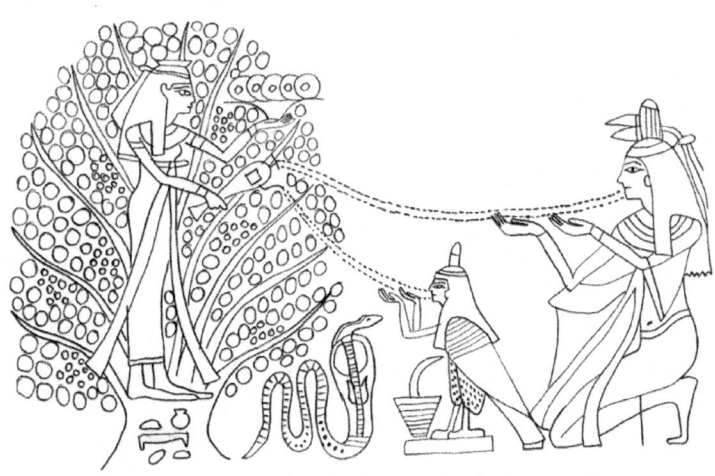

Goddess Hathor and the World Tree of Life symbolism (inspired by ancient Egyptian art).

Ancient Greece also had a charming group of woodland deities called nymphs who inhabited trees, rocks, stones, and water. There were different kinds of tree nymphs: Caryatides were walnut nymphs, Heliconians were willow nymphs, Meliae were ash nymphs, and Dryads were oak nymphs. (Later in history, all tree nymphs were called Dryads.) Sometimes, the nymphs had a group spirit as well. For example, Melia, the group spirit of the ash nymphs, held the wisdom of the whole ash family whereas the individual Meliae spirit animated a single tree. Like most legendary elementals, nymphs lived in another, more ethereal realm and visited ours only occasionally.

The god of the wilderness, Pan, was a group spirit of the individual pans and his Roman counterpart Faunus was the father of fauns. One of Pan's attributes was the pine tree, and people ceremonially burned fires near these trees to evoke him. Pine also links to god Attis who was transformed into a pine tree after his death (this legend relates to the Egyptian Osiris and his entombment in a tamarisk tree).

The Greek writer Hesiod wrote that humans were "the fruit of an ash tree," which evokes the Norse myth of the first man being made from an ash tree. Another curious example of tree worship can be seen in the custom of planting a personal life tree upon a baby's birth. As well as guarding the individual, these life trees also guarded cities and oracles. The destiny of the tree was believed to mirror the destiny of the person or place. This tradition was adopted by the Romans, and the founding tree of Rome was the fig tree under which a caring she-wolf reared Romulus and Remus.

The Roman poet Virgil (Publius Vergilius Maro) wrote that in ancient times, forests used to belong to natural devas such as nymphs and fauns, and the first, primitive people lived among them. Once again, there is that mind-boggling belief that these first people were born of tree trunks. The question is: Was this meant literally or as a symbolic reference to the World Tree of Life that pertains to all living organisms?

Japanese folklore has its own tree nymphs called Kodama who protect sacred trees. They are believed to either inhabit individual trees or roam around the woods. The elders knew which trees had a Kodoma spirit in them and thus protected them from harm. In Thai mythology, we meet with woodland nymphs called Nang Mai meaning the "ladies of the wood." Like the Greek nymphs, there are more types of Nang Mai such as the spirit of the grand ta-khian trees called Nang Ta-khian or the Nang Tani that guard banana trees.

The descendants of the Incas, the Q'ero people, still revere the Cosmic Mother or Mother Earth, and natural deities such as the spirits of trees, *malque,* or the spirits of the rainbow, *kuichi.* They believe that mountain devas called *apus* protected them from the invasion of Spanish armies by causing earthquakes and landslides. They also believe in the spirits of the four basic elements and the mysterious fifth element that pertains to *achachle* meaning "the omnipresent and all-permeating spirit." The spiritual leaders of the Q'ero, who were both male and female, were able to connect to all these natural spirits. There is also a correlation to the Egyptian and Mesopotamian sun gods as their mythology mentions that their father, Inkarri or Inca (like the empire of the same name), was the son of the sun and founded the city of Cusco by throwing down a golden staff.

In Old Ireland, the sun god Lugh was believed to exist in another dimension and live beside a golden tree. There's also the legend of Avalon, originally Afallon, which translates as "the isle of apple trees." The Irish Arthurian legends mention this mysterious island as a place of eternal spring and summer where trees flower and bear fruit simultaneously. Queen Argante rules there with her group of female healers. Moreover, some Celtic tribes were named after sacred trees: the Eburones were the tribe of yew, the Lemovices the tribe of elm, and the Fir Bile the tribe of the sacred tree.

The Celtic and Germanic god of the wild, Cernunnos, was associated with an oak tree, and on the ancient Gundestrup cauldron he is portrayed as holding a serpent in one hand and a disk in the other, the two symbols most commonly depicted with the World Tree of Life (see picture). In the Indian Pashupati seal, we find a four-faced deity similar to Cernunnos. He's also horned, sits in a similar meditative position, and is, too, surrounded by wild animals. Cernunnos could also be a counterpart to the mysterious four-faced Mesopotamian god from the cylinder seal and the Slavic Svetovid or Czech Svantovít who were also portrayed with four faces. The Slavs erected wooden pillars in honor of this primordial god, and some historians speculate that he later became Saint Vitus.

Cernunnos as depicted on the Gundestrup cauldron.

The god of the wild (drawing inspired by the Sumerian cylinder seal).

The ancient Indian god of the wild (possibly Brahma), inspired by Pashupati seal art.

Another Celtic legend says that the wizard Merlin climbed the tree of wisdom and knowledge, the Pine of Barenton, and hasn't returned into the world of mortal men since. Some think that Merlin is asleep in the sacred tree, waiting to be reawakened, but the legend might just as well be describing Merlin's shamanic journey through the World Tree of Life. His story would then correlate to that of Gautama Buddha or god Odin who also found great wisdom by a tree.

Interestingly, even during the medieval Christianization of Europe, the Church adopted some pagan traditions, and the forest and tree devas were preserved in the unified entity of the Green Man, or sometimes the Green Woman, that represents the power of trees and woodlands.

Roman historian Tacitus described the ancient Germanic tribes as very peaceful people who lived in wild woodlands, which were their homes as well as sacred shrines. They were even believed to be descended from the god of the earth, Tuisto. In Norse mythology, the human race was created by god Odin and his two brothers Vili and Vé from trees. The first man, Ask, was created from an ash tree and the first woman, Embla, from an elm (some interpretations claim it might have been vine or elder). Similarly, in Irish legends, the first man was created from alder and the first woman from rowan.

Like Guatama Buddha, god Odin found enlightenment and wisdom by a tree. Legends say that he hung himself upside down on the World Tree, Yggdrasil, and journeyed to the well of Mímir – Mímir being the god of ancestral memory – where he received the magic of the runes, which he then shared with the other gods and with mankind.

In Norse mythology, the nature deities were known as the Vanir. Two of them were siblings Freya and Freyr who mirror the Lithuanian earth mother Zemyna and her brother Zemininkas.

The Slavic Leshy (or Leszy in Polish and Lešij in Czech) is a male spirit of the woodland that can be scary to those who mistreat the local flora and fauna. If he dislikes someone, he chases them away with various tricks or with his terrifying roars. Although he may change shape and size, he usually appears as a horned giant, and that's why he has been compared to the Celtic Cernunnos, Greek Pan, or Roman Faunus. Leshy was also believed to have a wife, Leshachikha, and children they called Leshonki. His name was preserved in the Czech word for forest: *lesy*.

There's also a woodland guardian in the mountain region that separates Poland and Czechia (the Czech Republic) called Karkonosz in Polish or Krakonoš in Czech who majestically roams the wilderness supported by his mighty tree staff. This mythical figure was actually the inspiration for J. R. R. Tolkien's wizard Gandalf.

A being similar to Krakonoš or Lešij can be found in Estonian mythology under the name of Metsaisa. He was also a gigantic woodland deity who knew the language of the wild animals and guarded the wilderness. He punished those who treated the local beings wrongfully but helped the ones who respected his natural kingdom.

The most venerated trees among the ancient Slavs were the oak, which was considered to be the god tree, and the linden, which was seen as the goddess tree. Archeological excavations proved that there were many sacred oak and linden groves in the Bohemian regions where the Slavs settled after the Germanic and Celtic tribes moved to the west and north. The primordial Slavic god Rod, who was probably later replaced by Perun, Svarog, and Svantovid, was depicted in symbolic form as a spiked wheel, which is one of the ancient symbols of the natural cycles and the World Tree of Life. Curiously, the word *rod* means "kin" in Czech and the Proto-Slavic word *rod* means "nature" or "harvest." Is it a coincidence that in English it stands for another symbol for the World Tree of Life, the rod or, in other words, the staff?

The Baltic spirits of the woodlands were the Laumės. These

devas liked to dance beside streams, swamps, and ponds, and often left curious rings in the soil, grass, or fields. They are counterparts to the Slavic Vilas or Rusalkas, the graceful nymphs who liked to dance in sacred groves, by ponds, and in meadows. The Laumės appeared in the form of female goats or as women with goat hooves. They shared attributes with the archetypal females, the Fates, Norns, or Sudice, as they were often spotted in a group of three and were known for their spinning and weaving skills as well as for predicting the destiny of children upon their births.

The miscellaneous devas emerging and turning into trees could be simply interpreted as fabricated mythological figures who never existed, or they could be actual beings who traveled between our world and the others through tree portals or the axis mundi of the World Tree of Life.

It's quite fascinating that various ancient cultures shared the belief that not only deities but also animals and humans actually descended from trees. This was most likely an allegory for the unity of all beings in one ever-growing World Tree of Life. However crazy it may sound, though, we do share some characteristics with trees.

Like trees, we stand upright with arms and legs stemming from our central trunk. Our arteries, veins, and capillaries bifurcate like branches or leaf veins. Our blood could be compared to the tree sap and our circulatory system to the tiny tubes that pump water from tree roots to branches. Tree bark protects these tubes like our skin protects our cardiovascular system. Just as we bleed if wounded, sap oozes from a tree when harm is done, which is why pruning is not advised during the early springtime when the sap rises back to the branches. Furthermore, the tubular branching pattern of our lungs resembles the branch and root system of trees.

A more symbolic correlation is the resemblance between the double helix of DNA molecules and the ancient symbol of the caduceus, which also contains symbolism of the World Tree of Life. Another fascinating fact is that while we breathe in oxygen and breathe out carbon dioxide, trees take in carbon dioxide and release oxygen, and that's what creates the wonderful harmony between us.

Like all living beings on this planet, trees are dependent on the energy of the sun and water. Trees are collectors of solar energy, and they harvest it by converting it into bonds of sugar molecules. They then transport nutrients from the mycalea organisms through their roots and give them carbon in exchange, creating a beautiful synchronization in woodlands. However, trees not only consume water but also produce it. Water is transported through the ground via roots into the branches, and water then evaporates from the tiny pores on leaves or needles into the sky to become rain.

Trees also communicate with each other, though in a very different way than us: They share information through an underground system of roots and mycelia. If some trees are missing nutrients, they send out signals and other trees help them out. Trees even recognize their kin. The mother trees, the oldest and biggest trees in a certain area, communicate with their descendants even from a distance of many miles and send them nutrition.

4

Tree Staff:

The Conduit of Tree Magic

In previous chapters, we have focused on the World Tree of Life and its reoccurring symbolism in mythology, legend, shamanism, religion, and philosophy. We have also established that it could be viewed as the life force as well as the interdimensional light body of the planet, which manifests in the electromagnetic field. This natural, protective field resembles a torus that shields our planet from radiation and other harmful influences.

The central vortex of spiraling energy belonging to the electromagnetic field and the torus could be seen as the axis mundi, the world pole, the shamanic tunnel, or the celestial ladder that unites all the dimensions of this planet, other celestial bodies, and even galaxies. The vortex resembles a tree trunk as well as its magical representation – the staff.

In shamanism and magic, the staff is the epitome of tree energy, especially its trunk. Therefore, it shouldn't come as a surprise that the legendary staffs, rods, and wands of deities, wise women and men, prophets, or rulers shared common symbolism with the World Tree of Life.

Moreover, a tree staff helps us connect with our life force, our Tree of Life, and our light bodies, which makes it a powerful support during journeys into the otherworldly realms, especially if the tree that the staff came from has an interdimensional portal. In magic and shamanism, tree staffs have also been used as shields and to cast away negative forces. It's quite fascinating how united the tree and staff symbolism is in diverse ancient cultures from all over the world.

There are assorted examples of magic staffs from ancient Egypt, Mesopotamia, and Etruria. The curved tree staff called *gamlu* was a magical tool of the Mesopotamian gods Marduk and Amurru as well as sages called *apkallu* who were depicted with bird or fish-like features. The gamlu staff was used for exorcising evil spirits and purifying energies. There's a clear resemblance between the gamlu and the Egyptian *heka*, a crooked staff often seen in the hands of deities and pharaohs. The heka probably had the same magical purpose and must have been more than just a symbol of dominion as commonly interpreted. The heka was often seen diagonally crossing another staff or rather a flail called *nekhakha*.

The Egyptian was-scepter staff had a forked bottom and curved top, and both ends could have represented the heavenly arc.

However, there's also a similarity to the Norse rune Uruz, the mother rune of creation, vitality, and strength (see chapter eight).

The top of the was-scepter was carved with the features of an unknown animal head that probably represented the Bennu bird. The Bennu bird was an important bird deity who created itself and perpetually regenerated on the top of the acclaimed Persea Tree, which was the Egyptian Tree of Life. This renewing quality links to another animal pertaining to the tree and staff symbolism – the serpent. It also evokes the self-sustaining quality of the torus and the electromagnetic field.

Bennu was a solar deity and was sometimes described as the sun itself, while at other times it personified gods such as Atum or Osiris. Furthermore, it was known to banish darkness and welcome spirits into the afterlife. Bennu was probably an inspiration for the Greek phoenix who was, too, associated with perpetual rebirth, and sun and fire symbolism.

Some historians believe that the animal head on top of the was-scepter represents *sha*, the animal of god Seth, but it could be the Bennu bird just as well due to the wing-like shape on top of its head and the fact that magic staffs were often accompanied by avian beings (see picture).

The was-scepter was often seen in the hands of the creator deities such as god Ptah who thought the world into existence based on his heart's desire and materialized it with the use of magical words; the god Atum who, like the Bennu bird, created himself and completed the manifestation of the world; and goddess Seshat, who was described as "the one who wrote first." Not only deities but also pharaohs and sometimes craftsmen were depicted with this staff.

Bennu bird (inspired by various Egyptian artworks).

The was-scepter detail in comparison with the Seth animal
(from left to right).

In various reliefs and artifacts, the was-scepter staff was depicted together with the ankh cross and the djed pillar, which is the Egyptian axis mundi. Curiously, all these symbols were sometimes stylized into a half-human body. There's also a strange example of a scepter securing an unidentified entity, which might represent its spirit-banishing quality (see picture). We could deduce that all three symbols were conduits between the physical world and the other dimensions, especially the djed pillar, or World Pillar.

Ancient Egyptian god Ptah with his staff that unites the was-scepter, ankh, and djed pillar. (Inspired by an ancient Egyptian relief.)

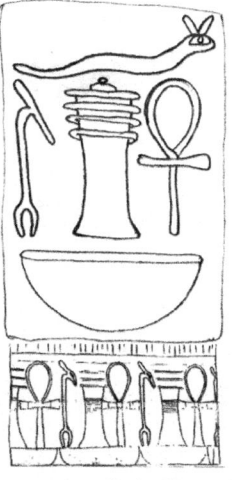

The was-scepter, djed pillar, and ankh were often depicted together and with a serpent.

An interesting ankh figure holding two was-scepters. (Inspired by an ancient Egyptian relief.)

A curious example of a humanoid was-scepter taming a demon-like being. (Inspired by an ancient Egyptian relief.)

Many archeological excavations proved that the was-scepters were actually made of tree branches. Mystic, author, and expert on Egyptian mysticism René Adolphe Schwaller de Lubicz considered the was-scepter a symbol of a living branch that represented the magical powers of trees. In his book *The Egyptian Miracle*, he called the was-scepter "the flux of the Word, the vivifying sap." The mention of the Word could hint at the magical words that god Ptah uttered to manifest the world based on his loving thoughts. And the prominent attributes of this creator god were none other than the was-scepter, the ankh, and the djed pillar, which were all bound together on his staff (see picture).

The tradition of the was-scepter was preserved as a symbol of dominion in the hands of rulers and religious figures in various cultures. However, the magic-related purpose was probably obscured and unknown to the public.

The ancient Greeks portrayed deities and respected elders, judges, leaders, and priests with staffs and scepters. The Greek gods Dionysus and Bacchus had a staff with a pinecone atop called a *thyrsus*. Interestingly, the pinecone can be seen on top of the pope's scepter to this day. Pinecones alone were depicted in the hands of Mesopotamian gods, suggesting that pine was a revered tree or that it represented the third eye that is believed to be located in the pineal gland, which itself resembles a pinecone. The ancient Phoenician scarab corpus amulets show many gods and goddesses with staffs that had a pinecone atop. The pine could be a link to the eternal World Tree of Life as pines never shed their leaves.

The Etruscan and later Roman staff *lituus* had a distinctly curved edge. There's an interesting avian correlation to it because it was a magic staff of the augurs, the diviners who practiced augury, which means conveying the will of deities by studying birds, their behavior, and flight. The lituus was sometimes curled into a spiral or a serpent head and thus the bird and serpent meet again. Strangely, the word "lituus" was later used as a name for a curved trumpet as well.

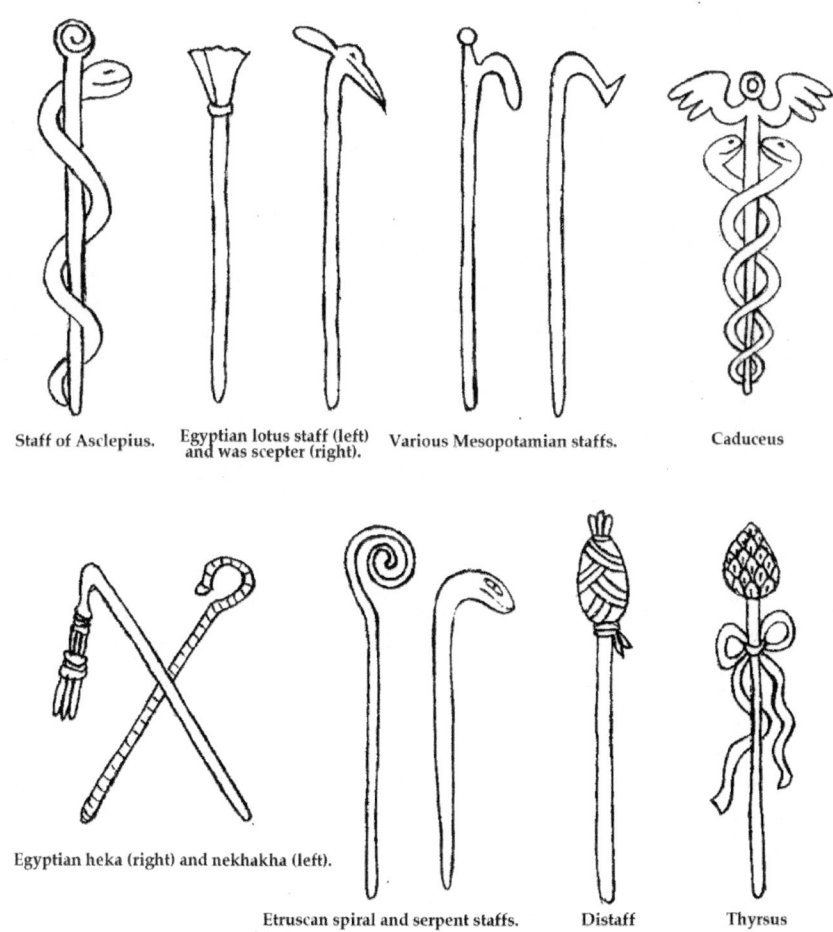

Staff of Asclepius. Egyptian lotus staff (left) and was scepter (right). Various Mesopotamian staffs. Caduceus

Egyptian heka (right) and nekhakha (left). Etruscan spiral and serpent staffs. Distaff Thyrsus

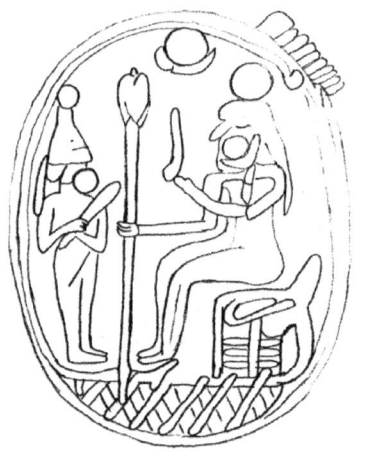

Figure holding a staff (inspired by the Phoenician scarab corpus).

God Amurru holding the gamlu staff as depicted on the Mesopotamian cylinder seal.

Thyrsus

Etruscan lituus staff (drawing inspired by ancient Etruscan art).

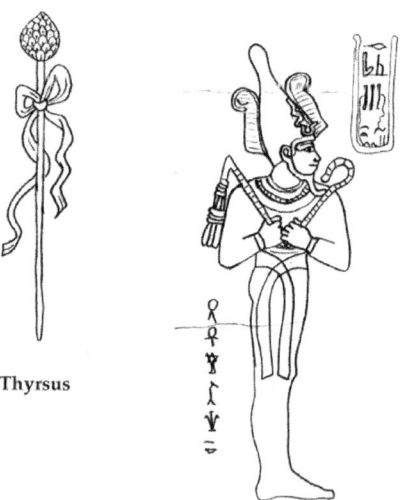

God Osiris holding two magic scepters: heka and nekhakha.

The Roman goddess Victory had a staff with an eagle head (*aquila*), and a staff with a serpent, dragon, or eagle head was also carried by the *draconarius*, a signifier in the Roman army. The Persian prophet Zoroaster was depicted holding a staff, which sometimes burned and looked more like a torch and could refer to the light phenomena sightings that were recorded near to sacred trees in ancient times.

Throughout ancient history, tree staffs have been used for healing, have helped with divination, and have provided creative inspiration. The Celtic god Dagda had a staff that killed with one end and healed with the other. The Celtic bards carried staffs made of hazel, a magical tree that was believed to ignite a poetic inspiration called *awen*. In fact, the Celts never burned or felled hazel and always asked the tree whether they could take its wood before they cut a piece of its branch. In East Sussex, England, there's an intriguing hill figure called the Long Man of Wilmington that is depicted holding two staffs. The figure is believed to have been created during the Iron Age, but some historians suggest that it is from the 16th century.

The Germanic and Norse god Woden (Odin in Old Norse) carried a spear staff called *Gungnir* that was carved with the runes, the sacred codes he received during his shamanic journey to the well of ancestral wisdom at the roots of the World Tree. Staffs inscribed with runes were found all over Scandinavia and the Netherlands. Some Germanic seeresses were even named after their magic staffs. The name of seeress Waluburg comes from *waluz* which in Old German means "magical staff." And the name of seeress Ganna derives from the Old Norse *gandr* that translates as "magic wand."

Sometimes, magic staffs were also found alone. An interesting example is a 10th-century yew staff found buried vertically in a swamp in Hemdrup, Denmark. The staff had serpent-like and scale-like shapes inscribed on it, along with various symbols, runes, animals, a human figure, and a triquetra. Another peculiar pine staff that bore runic symbols for exorcising disease was found in Denmark and dates to the 13th century.

In Northern Europe, staffs were common attributes of female deities and authoritative figures called völva, which actually means "a staff woman." Excavations have unearthed highly venerated women buried with staffs. Some historical sources suggest that these staffs were regarded as kitchen tools such as roasting spits or measuring sticks for handicrafts, but since they were visibly uneven and heavily ornamented, it seems unlikely. The völvas' staffs probably had magical purposes, and even though some of them were made of iron, their crooked shapes imitated tree branches. In her book, *Witches and Pagans*, author Max Dashu points out that the ornaments often made the völva staffs look like distaffs. She further links these distaffs to the attributes of the ancient spinners of destiny usually pertaining to the World Tree of Life called Norns, Fates, Parceas, Moires, Sudice, and so forth.

An interesting völva was found in Veka, Hordaland, Norway. She was buried in a position that looked as if she were flying on what seemed to be a distaff. This peculiar völva is reminiscent of European legends and fairy tales about witches roaming the sky on staffs, broomsticks, or later along boundary lines. Who knows whether these stories conceal the awareness of astral travel?

In legend and mythology, we find many deities or esteemed females with magic staffs or distaffs. An illustrious Sardinian seeress, Lughia Rajosa, had a magical distaff that guarded her property and whistled when intruders were around. The distaff was also an attribute of the Norse goddess Frigg who was believed to spin the clouds in Orion's Belt. The constellation was known to the Norse people as *Friggerock* which translates as "Frigg's spinning wheel."

A golden distaff called *chryselokatos* was one of the main symbols of the Greek goddess Artemis and a similar distaff also belonged to goddess Athena, though it was later replaced by a spear. Besides the staff, Athena's attributes were the olive tree, a serpent, and an owl – symbols that usually pertain to the World Tree of Life (tree, serpent, avian being). Other spinning female personalities were goddesses Minerva, Laima, and Brigid. The goddess of divine justice, Nemesis, carried an apple branch and a spiked wheel. Sometimes the wheel was replaced by an ash branch; nevertheless, both the staff and wheel are common representations of the World Tree of Life.

All these spinning goddesses share attributes with the Norns, the giantesses who spin the world's destiny at the roots of the Yggdrasil and carve runes into the trunk. The spinning wheel has sometimes been regarded as the spiked wheel, wheel of the year, or wheel of seasonal changes, and the distaffs have been interchangeable with other staffs.

The symbolism of spinning wheels and distaffs was preserved throughout the Middle Ages in art and tradition. The depictions of women in the act of spinning or weaving was a popular artistic theme back then, and there was even a Catholic holiday called Saint Distaff Day celebrated annually on January 7, which marked the end of the twelfth day of Christmas and the beginning of a new cycle.

Despite the perpetuation of distaff symbolism, the tree staff was the first magic tool that was prohibited during the strict Catholic Christianization in Europe. Freedom and the power of the individual diminished, and the magic staffs turned into scepters of dominion in the hands of rulers and religious authorities. Original and true Christianity, however, knew well of the staff's true meaning and purpose as magic staffs appear in many biblical stories in the hands of prophets, patriarchs, and saints.

Miracles performed with tree staffs were often associated with the water element. For example, Saint Berthe used her staff to make a sacred fountain flow in the direction of her home. Moses used his almond staff, which was also called the "rod of God" to extract water from stones and even used it to part the Red Sea. Irish legends say that one day Saint Patrick thrust his staff on a rock and water poured out. This story also mirrors an ancient Celtic belief that a well appears where a fairy's staff touches the soil.

There are also Christian tales about staffs turning into trees, which was regarded as a holy sign. The Bible mentions that God instructed Moses to take one staff from each of the twelve competing tribes and whichever tribe's staff sprouted first would then start the religious leadership. Aaron's tribe of Levi won because his staff blossomed overnight, turning into an almond tree.

The biblical patriarch Jacob crossed the River Jordan supported by his staff and healed cattle with its help. Saint Christopher carried the baby Jesus over a stream and God told him to plant his staff in the ground so that it could one day become a tree. Another example of a magic staff turning into a holy tree can be found in the English legend of the holy thorn tree in Glastonbury, which grew from the staff of Joseph of Arimathea, a loyal supporter of Jesus Christ who planted it there after voyaging to England in the 1st century AD.

Another biblical story mentions how Mamre, Abraham's shepherd, thrust his staff into the ground where it turned into an oak tree that was held in high regard from that time forward. However, there's also a legend that says the oak sprang from the staff of Abraham's angelic visitor. Abraham lived by the oak and was later buried there as well.

All shepherds had their staffs and therefore even Jesus Christ, who was regarded as the shepherd of men, had one. Like the was-scepter of the Egyptian deities and rulers, his staff was depicted with a curved end. Most say that such staffs were used to herd cattle, but there could be a deeper connection. Given the biblical stories and magical connotations, it's certainly not just the conventional shepherd symbolism that links Jesus Christ to a tree staff.

Brigid with a distaff by Ivana Axman.

The art of spinning
(inspired by medieval illustrations).

Jesus holding a staff
(drawing inspired by a mosaic from
Devon cathedral).

Etruscan lituus staff
(drawing inspired by ancient
Etruscan artwork).

Woman with a distaff
(inspired by a drawing by
Albrecht Durer).

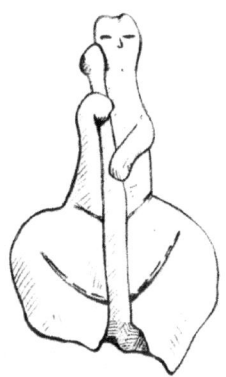

A goddess holding a staff or a serpent (inspired by one of the figurines found in the shrine of Sabatynivka in Ukraine).

Ancient goddess/venerated horned deity holding a staff (inspired by a 1st-century relief found in a Roman fort in Northumbria, UK).

Goddess Hathor with a wadj scepter (inspired by ancient Egyptian artwork).

A mysterious bird-headed woman holding a tree-like staff (inspired by the 10th-century Manx stone cross on the Isle of Man).

Besides avian beings, the World Tree of Life and its magic mediator, the tree staff, was often accompanied by a serpent. Mesopotamian goddess Inanna (also known as Ishtar) had a staff with two serpents coiled around it. The staff of goddess Demeter had a single serpent, but a pair of winged serpents pulled her chariot. Ancient Greek healer Asclepius used his serpent-entwined magic staff to treat his patients. This staff is used to this day as a symbol of healthcare, hospitals, and medicine. It is, however, often confused with the caduceus, the staff of Hermes (Roman Mercury), who was likewise believed to use it for healing and for guiding souls into the afterlife.

The caduceus unites the two animal guardians of the World Tree of Life – the serpent and the bird, which is here represented by wings. Both these animals symbolize movement. The serpent is the tree's vitality and the bird is the freedom of its spirit. The staff of god Osiris was similar to the caduceus as it also had two entwined serpents, but the top had a pinecone instead of wings.

Sometimes, staffs turned into serpents and vice versa. A good example can be found in the biblical story of how Aaron and his brother Moses proved to the pharaoh that they could truly speak to God by casting Aaron's staff to the floor where it became a serpent. In fact, many ancient artifacts show deities holding serpents instead of staffs. The Egyptian goddess Isis was often portrayed holding a cobra as a staff, and so was the Canaan fertility goddess Qetesh. The statuettes of goddesses and priestesses in ancient Crete usually held two serpents, and similar figures were also found in Hera's temple in Argos. And on the most famous depiction of the Celtic god of the wilderness, Cernunnos, we see him grasping a serpent in one hand.

Staff of Osiris.

Goddess Innana (aka Ishtar) with her serpent staff (inspired by ancient Mesopotamian art).

Goddess Demeter with a serpent coiled around her staff (inspired by a Roman statue from the 2nd century.)

Augur serpent staff (inspired by an Etruscan fresco from the 6th century.)

Asclepius with his serpent staff (inspired by an ancient Roman statue).

5

Bird and Serpent:

The Guardians of the Tree and Staff

As mentioned in the previous chapters, birds and serpents have a strong affiliation with the World Tree of Life. Serpents mainly preside over the roots, as the shapes of roots are serpentine in nature. Birds have their dominion in the branches because they like to perch and nest in tree crowns. Both the bird and serpent have their own archetypal meaning in the World Tree of Life, but in the most symbolic sense we could say they represent the unity between the celestial and earthly realms. Both these animals are powerful mediators between the dimensions of the World Tree of Life and thus make irreplaceable spirit guards and guides on the path of tree magic.

Let's first focus on the archetypal meaning of the serpent. In ancient mythology and legend, serpents have been linked to vitality, healing, shielding, spiritual knowledge, wisdom, ancestry, and awakening.

For example, the Indian god Shiva has been depicted with one or more snakes that represent his wisdom and power beyond the limitations of the dual world including time and space. Before Siddhartha reached his Buddhahood, he was protected from harmful storms by Mucalinda, the king of the benevolent serpentine beings called Nagi. The Nagi were believed to live in underground kingdoms; they were more advanced than humans and therefore rarely accessible to them.

Moreover, the Navajo tradition has a snake that shape-shifts into human form to give people healing advice. Sometimes, serpents were even considered our ancestors. Fuxi and Nuwa were the Chinese half-human, half-serpentine deities who created man out of clay. In ancient artwork, like the Nagi, this serpentine couple can be seen entwined, which suggests a connection to the two serpents in the various magic staffs.

To many indigenous African tribes, serpents are wise beings who transmit messages between ancestors and descendants. In Lithuania and the Baltic regions, snakes were known as the benevolent guardians of homes, family, and the whole kin. To this day, they are depicted on village houses as mascots, and if a snake takes shelter under someone's house, it's a sign of good luck. Ancestors, sacred beings, and even deities were believed to manifest as serpents at times, and therefore a strong superstition developed. No harm should be done to the snake that lived beneath someone's house otherwise the whole family could be shattered.

The Slavs called their home snake Domovoj, and before their houses were built, a sacred space was established for Domovoj under the threshold. Domovoj was not only seen as the guardian of the home, but he was also considered a human ancestor. Sometimes he took the shape of a wise old man and was called "grandfather snake."

As I was writing this book, I discussed this research with my mom, and she told me that her grandparents still kept the tradition of offering milk and honey to snakes in February. She said snakes were invited to settle under the thresholds of the house, and their presence heralded the brightest part of the year as well as the rising of a tree's sap into its branches. It's quite intriguing that February, the time when sap starts pumping up from a tree's roots into its branches, is the time when serpents begin to ascend from their underground shelters.

Moreover, February 1 is the Day of Serpents in Lithuania, a festival during which serpents return to the villages from the woods, heralding the brightest months of the year. On the other hand, when the snakes depart in the fall, the darkest time begins. Isn't it beautiful how the snakes clearly mark the light and dark halves of the year? February 1 is also the day of Imbolc, the Celtic holiday that celebrates the first signs of spring, the fire element – the sun – and the final dawning of the brightest days. It's also the holiday of the swan goddess Brigid. Like snakes, swans are known to return from the south in February. And let me share one more interesting fact: The Lithuanian word *gyvatė* means both snake and life force.

In ancient Greece and Rome, serpents guarded temples and shrines. The cults of Juno or Athena were known for having snake-feeding festivals for the snakes that lived in the cave under the sanctuaries. It's quite interesting that during the Catholic Christianization period in Europe, the gathering in groves was forbidden and serpents were demonized. An Irish medieval legend tells of Saint Patrick casting his staff on a serpent and splitting the animal into four parts. This was probably symbolic for destroying the serpent and casting it into the four main elements or the four worldly directions. The serpent was banished as an evil tempter, and its true legacy was disregarded. On the other hand, Christianity has always been very well aware of malevolent reptilian beings and has a good, proven method to guard against their wickedness and manipulation.

The truth of the matter is that even in pre-Christian times, serpents were either considered the guardians or the enemies of the World Tree of Life. Perhaps it was so because they represented both the life and death cycle as, after all, some snakes can be deadly poisonous. Most ancient cultures were aware of both the life-giving side of serpents as well as the life-threatening one. Apep, the ancient Egyptian entity that combined serpent, dragon, and crocodile features was considered a god of chaos and all evil. He was also the enemy of justice, balance, and order – the virtuous values represented by goddess Maat and god of light Ra who was known to defeat Apep. There are many legends of heroes and gods killing serpents or dragons. The Greek hero Hercules killed Ladon, the Norse god Thor slew Jörmungandr, and the Hindu god Indra destroyed Vritra.

Modern shamans are still aware of reptilian demons that try to trick or possess human minds. In his book, *The Way of the Shaman*, author Michael Harner describes how he was taught to banish such a demon with a magic staff carved with geometric symbols of protection. His shamanic guide told him that the staff was more powerful than any weapon, and he experienced this soon after when he encountered a reptilian demon in the wild. Miraculously, it was enough for him to hold the staff in front of his body for the demon to vanish.

Perhaps that's why serpents have often been depicted in pairs, entwined around the World Tree of Life or magic staffs – like everything in this world, they pertain to the dualistic games between life and death, dark and light, good and evil.

It's important to mention that in various ancient cultures, serpents were attributes of the goddess. The goddesses Marša, Mara, Fate, Laima, and Celtic Verbeia were often depicted holding snakes, and the Greek goddess Athena had a flying serpent who guarded the Acropolis and was fed honey cakes by the locals. Curious examples of women with serpent-like legs have been found in Denmark and Germany dating back to the Bronze Age. Some of these had either serpentine bodies from the waist down or a fishtail, hence the Melusine and other mermaid-like beings.

The cow also joined the serpent in the representation of the goddesses. The Greek goddess Hera whom Homer called "cow-faced" had serpent votive figures in her temples, and the depictions of the Egyptian cow-headed goddess Hathor often show her holding serpents. Isn't it interesting how, over time, both cow and snake have been used as insults for women, and the sacred animals and symbols of the goddess have become shameful?

Another archetypal animal pertaining to the World Tree of Life and staff is the bird. While serpents epitomize the earthly powers and realms, birds rule over the celestial dimensions. They remind us of our spirit's detachment and freedom but are also believed to transmit messages between the worlds.

Birds have not been demonized like serpents because they have always represented the spirit and heaven. That's why the sacredness of the birds, especially the dove, was perpetuated throughout the Middle Ages. This is quite logical, as in medieval Christian philosophy, the heavenly realms were considered pure and ideal while the earthly ones, occupied by the serpent, were seen as faulty and unworthy (not to mention the hellish view of the netherworld). The soul's ascension to heaven was the main focus and the earth was ignored, but what happens when we cut a tree crown from its roots?

Bronze Age Europe depicted miscellaneous bird-headed figures, and these were mainly found in shrines and groves. Many ancient deities were portrayed as roaming the heavens on avian beings. The Greek god Apollo and goddess Aphrodite rode on the back of their swans, Hermes drove a chariot pulled by roosters, and the Indian god of justice, Shani, had a loyal raven or crow. Sometimes, even the deities themselves were winged, for example, the Mesopotamian Inanna, Aztec Huitzilopochtli, Egyptian Isis, Greek Nike and Eros. The biblical angels, particularly the Cherubim and Seraphim, were also depicted with wings, although in Jewish tradition they appear wingless.

Like serpents, birds were associated with the polarities of life and death. Some bird species such as vultures or crows were considered heralds of war and death while others like doves, swans, or eagles were seen as signs of heavenly guidance. The Syrian eagle goddess Artagatis was known for guiding souls to the celestial spheres, and in Judaism a sacred eagle was allegedly sent by God to summon the souls of the departed to the heavens. In ancient Sumer, the eagle was also viewed as an avian psychopomp who transferred souls into the afterlife. In Norse mythology, god Odin took the form of an eagle to convey a sacred drink known as the "mead of poetry" to Asgard. Odin also had two ravens who represented his ability to travel between the realms of the World Tree. Furthermore, the divine swan maidens, Valkyrie, collected the souls of the departed and brought them to the heavenly halls of Valhalla.

Swans have an intriguing connection to the serpent as they are both S-shaped and start with the letter S in the English language. They also both live at the roots of the Norse Yggdrasil, and we even see them together in the sky, as both the Swan and Serpent constellations guard the center of our galaxy. And the truth is that some mythological serpents had wings as well, for example, the assorted mythological dragons, the feathered serpents of Mesoamerican cultures, or the fiery flying serpents described in the Bible.

A fascinating connection between the tree, the bird, the serpent, and the human body is in the teachings of yoga. Here, the spine is the central channel for kundalini energy, and the two entwining serpents are the duality that unites all the chakras and leads to the enlightenment represented by the crown chakra, often depicted as an open lotus or wings. The kundalini serpents coiling around the spine have often been compared to the double helix of the DNA spiral and the caduceus staff.

Furthermore, if we combine two caduceus staffs, one facing up and the other down, the image resembles a vortex. And this takes us back to the axis mundi of the World Tree of Life, the electromagnetic field, and therefore the torus. Could the two serpents even symbolize the electrical and magnetic forces that flow outward from within and below from above, meeting in the central vortex?

We could conclude that the serpent symbolizes the life force, vitality, rejuvenation, and the earthly realms while the bird represents lightness, freedom, overview, and the celestial spheres. The serpent teaches us about the importance of roots, ancestry, and base while the bird reminds us that we are not bound to the past or the material world and that we, too, have wings. The serpent connects us with the nature realms and nature deities while the bird chirps the messages from our celestial guides and opens our mind to the intergalactic consciousness.

In a shamanic sense, the serpent and bird are the guardians of the World Tree of Life as well as our own Tree of Life. Both these archetypal animals are the guides whose clever, adaptable motion shows us a way through the lattice of this matrix back to the interdimensional beings we were born to be. Together, they inspire us to surpass the labyrinth of the mind and reach the endless spiral of the heart.

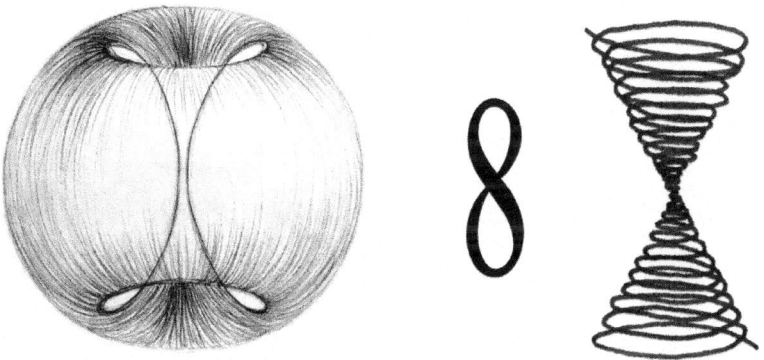

The central vortex of the torus –
a whirling, spiraling double cone, which also resembles
the figure-of-eight symbol of eternity.

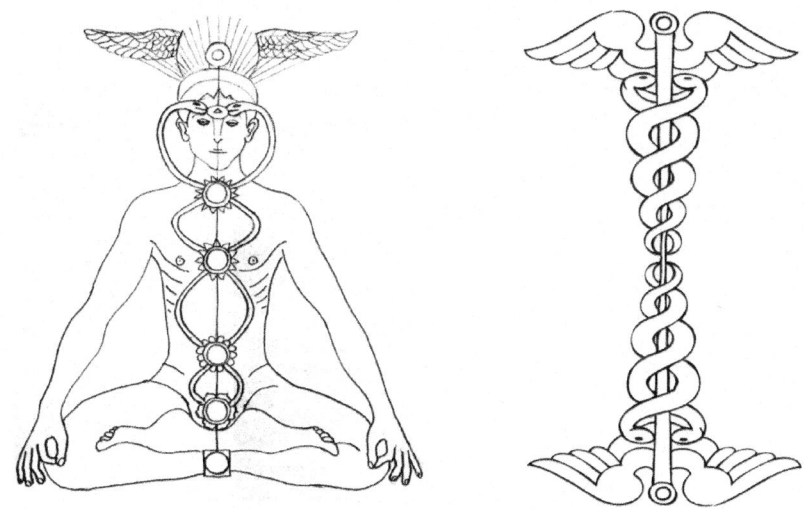

The caduceus mirrors the Kundalini (left)
and if we combine two caduceus staffs,
one facing up and the other down,
the image resembles a vortex (right).

# 6

Trees, Cycles, and Us

Trees in connection with spiked and solar wheels have been depicted since the Stone Age all over the world because together they represent the cycles of life. Like the Fates spinning the destiny of the world, the wheels of periodic change keep on turning. We may not be able to alter them, but we can learn how to work with them. The Fates, after all, not only master their inherent magical abilities but also the distaff, spindle, and spinning wheel, the power tools without which they wouldn't be able to spin the threads of destiny.

We all have a divine power beyond our ego that influences the spinning wheels of our fortune. The power tools, however, are not easily displayed to us; if they were, we wouldn't have so much fun finding them, would we? We need to decipher what these tools are and how to use them during our journey here on earth. Once we do that, we no longer spin on the perpetual cycles in the wheel of fortune but take hold of the power center like the Buddha did. The power center has often been symbolized by a tree staff as that is the symbolic axis of the World Tree of Life, the place of unity where we may finally understand what the wheels of ceaseless change are all about.

Once we find the true center and detach ourselves from the spinning wheels of karma, we become the spinner instead of the one who is being spun. The three Fates or Norns, after all, represent our magical potential in the trinity of the past, present, and future. It is in the center where we remember that we can be the creators, not just the creations.

Let's take a look at ancient spiked wheel symbolism from the perspective of the World Tree of Life and its toroidal electromagnetic field.

We could say that the torus is the three-dimensional representation of the circle. The torus unveils the movement or the cyclical motion of the circle. The crossed or star-shaped spikes symbolize the base of creation as well as the order within the wheel, therefore the seasons as well as the daily, monthly, and yearly cycles.

Cycles affect everything in this world and function like giant clocks that keep the same rhythm every day, every month, and every year. These rhythms create patterns that reflect in one another. The day and night cycles could be compared to the waning and waxing moon phases or the dark and light parts of the year.

The sun is symbolically reborn each dawn, as it is during the winter solstice, and could be compared to the new moon. The sun rises higher above the horizon in the morning, as it does during the spring equinox, and symbolically grows during the waxing moon phase. The noon sun echoes in the summer solstice when the sun is highest and in the full moon phase. The beautiful spectacles of the dusk reflect in the waning moon and the sun's decline during the autumn equinox. And just as the depth of the night cradles the new dawn or the new moon, the darkest days of the year promise the rebirth of the sun on the next winter solstice. The cycles help nature keep some order and avoid chaos. They reflect in one other, from the shorter to the longer, and create a beautiful fractal.

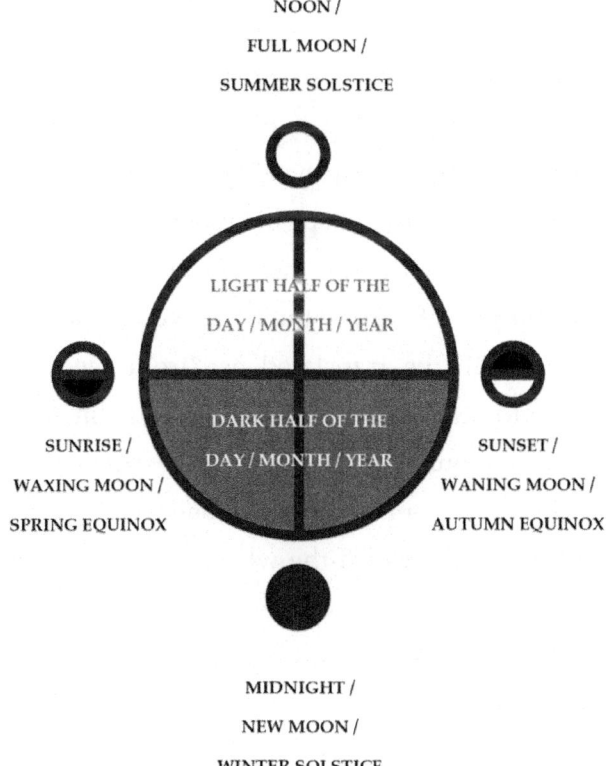

The cyclical motions of the earth around the sun, and the moon around the earth, were important to our ancestors who attuned to these perpetual cycles in order to understand what impact they had on the earth and, most importantly, what drove them. Observing plant life and trees helps us realize how beneficial the cycles are in the process of birth, growth, decay, and rebirth.

On a greater scale, the individual journey of a single tree starts, like our own, with a seed. As in the case of the chicken and the egg, we will never know whether the seed or the tree was first as they probably both exist as a prototype of creation. What we do know, however, is that in order to start growing, the seed first needs to develop strong roots, and the stronger the roots, the sturdier the tree. In our human lives, we also grow from our roots, family lineage, and background. Our base can make us stronger or weaker, so keeping our roots vital is a big challenge in our lives.

Undoubtedly, the most basic cycle of this world is the one from womb to tomb. Bronze Age European civilizations built their tombs in the shapes of wombs as they probably believed in the reincarnation concept of "from tomb to womb" as well. In tree symbolism, this could be translated as "from seed to tree" and "from tree back to seed." There are no endings in nature and its cycles, just a harmonious flow of continuous existence.

Many philosophies and religions believe in the cycles of reincarnation, and some regard the wheels of karma as a limitation that should be overcome. Eastern mystics strive to liberate their spirit from it by symbolically cutting the branches of attachment. What happens when we reach the freedom of enlightenment, though? Do we really surpass the karmic wheels of cause and effect or do we fall into another wheel instead? Judeo-Christian belief teaches us that Jesus Christ will liberate us from this earth and take us to our origins, our God. Gnosticism, on the other hand, sees this world as a product of the demiurge's charade that needs to be escaped. There are many ways, but all seem to lead to the same goal: freedom.

The concept of the World Tree of Life exceeds the cycles because in its branches and roots, all worlds coexist as simultaneous, eternal experiences. In its limitless reality, we may be able to surpass the cycles and travel through time or between the different realities. If we view the World Tree of Life as the symbolic torus of the electromagnetic field, and its vortex/axis mundi as the channel between the myriad of possibilities, suddenly all religions and philosophies begin to make more sense.

The ceaseless flow of the here and now certainly make us wonder whether we repeat certain cycles not only in this lifetime but also in other times and dimensions, and whether we may even relive some in order to correct them. Just as when a writer writes many drafts of a story before it feels right, or a painter makes varied sketches before completing a painting, our own magnum opus may take a few tries before it satisfies our spirit. Or as in the toroidal flow, we could all be ceaselessly improving ourselves and the worlds on a whole until we become part of a universal masterpiece.

Trees in Yearly, Monthly, and Daily Cycles

It's not a coincidence that serpents and birds have been linked to the World Tree of Life, as they represent the polarities and cycles of nature. Just as leaves fall from trees, snakes slough off their old skin twice or four times a year and birds shed old feathers and produce new ones at different stages of their lives and at different times of the year.

Snakes and birds are also known as the heralds of seasonal changes. Some birds relocate at the beginning of the winter and return in the springtime. Snakes, on the other hand, retreat underground during winter and return to the surface in the early spring when the sun begins its journey toward the highest point in the heavens and tree sap begins to rise into the branches.

On the whole, trees go through a huge change every spring. The tree's molecules react to the brighter days even before the temperatures rise, and the roots start to move sap up to the branches, preparing the tree for a new cycle of leafing. The tree sap, which is basically a revitalizing solution of water and minerals, descends back to the roots when the days become shorter and the tree enters a dormant phase, waiting for the next spring awakening. Conifers, however, transpire even in the wintertime, and so their sap continues flowing through the whole tree even during the cold months. That is probably one of the reasons why the yew tree was chosen to represent the World Tree of Life in Norse mythology.

Trees don't just react to yearly cycles but to lunar and daily cycles too. Even though the moon only reflects the sun's light, its luminosity affects nature more intensely because it's closer to our planet than the sun. The full moon generally brings more water, and that's why plants thrive during this phase. It's been proven that during the waxing moon, the soil is moister, seeds grow better, and tree sap rises more actively up to the branches and thus provides nourishment and supports growth. That's why during the full moon and waxing moon, tree fruit tends to be juicier. On the other hand, during the waning moon, sap moves more slowly and tends to descend to the roots, storing moisture in the underground system of roots where it absorbs nutrients. During the waning moon, there is less fluid in tree fruit, and it's therefore the best time to pick it for storage. It's also good to water trees more during this time.

As for the daily cycles, just as some plants tend to close up their leaves or flowers at night and open them up again in the morning, trees follow the sleep/wake pattern as well. In recent years, a team of researchers discovered that trees even tend to droop their branches and leaves slightly at night. Like us, trees are more vibrant in the light half of the day during the process of photosynthesis and calmer in the dark half of the day. And who knows, perhaps they even dream?

Us in Yearly, Monthly, and Daily Cycles

And how do the solar, lunar, and natural cycles relate to us? Would you believe that observing the cyclical changes in trees can be a profound inspiration for our own inner development? Trees, as well as humans, are affected by the continual exchange between the light and dark forces of nature. The perpetual changes are most visible in the branches and roots, which complement the central energy of the trunk. The wheels of cycles spin around and within us, and when we become aware of their purpose and go with them instead of against them, we thrive in harmony with the earthly and celestial realms.

Both our physical and mental bodies innately react to the daily sun cycles. Just as trees are busier during the day, soaking up the solar energy and releasing oxygen, we also tend to be more active during this time and receive, as well as give out, most of our energy then.

After sunset, a tree's energy descends to the roots, and we, too, naturally tend to focus inward. That's probably why some artists prefer creating in the evening or at night. The hustle and bustle of daily routines fades away, and the mind tunes in to the alpha waves. That's when contemplation, dreaming, and fantasizing becomes much easier.

It's been proven that from dawn to dusk, our mind works on a more conscious level than between dusk and dawn when our subconscious takes over the dominion. Although we may feel more mentally stimulated and active during the day, we connect better to our inner worlds at night, or during the in-between stages of the dusk and dawn when the conscious and subconscious minds meet.

Strangely, although the sun activates our pineal gland, the third eye, the effects can only be seen when it is dark around us, as that's when our inner light provides us with its guidance. That's why it's better to do meditations and journeys in darkness or at night. It's especially powerful to journey during the new moon phase or the dark half of the year.

The influence of the moon phases on our bodies and psyche has been widely studied, as our moods and energy levels tend to change during these periods. Just as the sap in trees moves faster during the full moon, we too are faced with a greater energy boost during that time. Everything intensifies when the moon is growing, and that energy is mirrored in our physical, mental, and emotional bodies. Some people may even experience irritation due to the enormous amount of energy reflected on our planet. Around the full moon, we may also feel less tired as the moonlight tends to draw us to it like a magnet.

And just as trees store moisture in their underground system around the dark half of the month, our energy shifts to the deeper, subconscious level at this time. Some people experience a lack of energy or feel more inward during the new moon as the nights are very dark. However, it's also a period during which we may reflect on our innermost selves and the light within. It's been observed that some people tend to be more intuitive, even psychic, around the new moon.

Like the sun cycles, the moon cycles can become a gateway to our inner alchemy if we are conscious of their deeper influence. We can absorb light during the bright periodicities and harvest it for the less luminous ones, thereby surpassing the outer darkness with the power of our inner light.

In the yearly cycle, the sun is symbolically born during the winter solstice and declines after the summer solstice, and together with the spring and autumn equinoxes, they create the solar cross. If we were to split the cross into two halves, we would notice that the light half of the year is between the spring equinox and the autumn equinox and the dark half is between the autumn equinox and the spring equinox. In a way, they mirror each other as well. It's all about the game between light and dark, the inner and outer worlds, the conscious and subconscious mind.

During the light part of the year, our conscious mind is more active, while our subconscious gains more dominion during the dark half of the year. The equinoxes are the magical in-between times when light and darkness achieve a perfect balance, which also motivates us to harmonize the subconscious and conscious parts of the mind.

Our ancestors honored the yearly cycles and celebrated the significant, dividing parts of the seasons. Some of these traditions have been preserved to this day. The pagan wheel of the year is represented by an eight-spoked wheel of two crosses. The basic cross consists of the two solstices – the winter solstice, Yule, and the summer solstice, Litha – and two equinoxes – the spring equinox, Ostara, and the autumn equinox, Mabon. The additional four festivals are believed to mark the times of the year when the veil between the ethereal and earthly realms is the thinnest. These are Imbolc (between the end of January and beginning of February), Beltane (between the end of April and beginning of May), Lammas (between the end of July and beginning of August), and Samhain (between the end of October and beginning of November). For this reason, these times provide wonderful opportunities for connecting with nature spirits, elves, and otherworldly realms.

Western civilization still keeps a few of these pagan traditions.

Christian culture applied some of them to their new system of faith: Yule became Christmas and Ostara, Easter. We still celebrate the symbolic New Year shortly after the new sun is born at the end of December. Tree symbolism has been preserved in the form of the Christmas tree, which unfortunately has become the worship of a dead tree instead of a living one. Rather than decorating trees in the wild like our ancestors used to, the tradition has changed to cutting them down, bringing them into our dwellings like a trophy, enjoying them for a couple of days, and throwing them away as soon as they begin to wither. Luckily, some people still prefer to buy living trees in pots that they can later plant outside.

The tree celebration is also reflected in the maypole tradition on May 1 when the brightest time of the year begins. During this festival, a wooden pole is carried around the neighborhood by a mysterious figure called the Green Man or Jack in the Green. This entity remained untamed even during medieval Catholic Christianization and gazes at us from church facades to this day. Originally, it was not just a pole that was celebrated, though; it was a living tree that was brought to the settlements. Once it was planted, its spirit was invoked and asked to protect the area.

Whether we attune to the yearly cycle or not, our bodies, minds, and souls are affected nevertheless. Our conscious mind, which could be compared to the tree branches, is more active during the light half of the year, while our subconscious, which could be compared to the tree roots, gains more power during the dark half. The times in between, therefore, around the spring and autumn equinoxes, is when the conscious and subconscious energies meet, and this often results in important insights or breakthroughs.

With the symbolic ascension of the sun, what has been hiding in the subconscious thus far may be brought into our conscious minds, challenging us to work with it. On the other hand, with the descent of the sun, our conscious efforts are properly incorporated and processed by the subconscious mind. Similarly, during the light part of the year, we tend to focus more on the outer world, and during the dark part, the inner worlds become more prominent. Since each person is different, though, it's best to pay attention to how we react individually to the solar and lunar cycles. Once we are in tune with our Tree of Life as well as the World Tree of Life, we become more aware of our growth during the earthly cycles and perhaps even the greater cycles beyond our comprehension.

It's important to note that trees and their reaction to cycles help us realize how important it is to balance polarities. Too much light would burn us and too much darkness would consume us. We need to reach a balance between light and shadow in order to thrive, and once we realize this, our shadow side stops being the enemy and may actually support our light side. Understanding the polarities of our Tree of Life helps us understand the World Tree of Life on a whole and vice versa.

Note: In the southern hemisphere, the light part of the year is from July to December, and the dark part of the year is from January to June.

PART II

PRACTICAL TREE MAGIC

This part of the book focuses mainly on working with our tree friends and the symbols, codes, and archetypes that represent them, as well as the concept of the World Tree of Life. It also suggests ways of harmonizing our Tree of Life, and therefore our life force and light body, with the World Tree of Life.

The following tree magic philosophies and practices are drawn from my own research and experiences, but are also inspired by the guidance I have received from my tree, animal, and otherworldly spirit guides.

7

Our Tree of Life

As mentioned in chapter two, the electromagnetic field of the earth mirrors the electromagnetic field of the heart. Our energy field therefore follows the same principle as our planetary energy field, which proves that we all have extraordinary self-sustaining and self-revitalizing abilities. Although our minds may not have caught up with the concept or we may not be open to its full potential, these abilities are integral to everything and everyone no matter what.

Of all the organs in the human body, the heart has the strongest electromagnetic field and is believed to have its own intelligence as well. Thanks to a discovery in 1991 by Dr.Armour, we know that the heart actually contains a small brain of its own. The brain, however, develops three months after the heart, and so we could say that the heart is not only the key to the body's mechanism, but also the original seed of its creation process.

By the mid-19th century, Baron Carl von Reichenbach had

already discovered the association between our electromagnetic field and our life force, which he called the Odic force. The Odic force and its study – odology – focuses on the properties of the life force that surrounds all living things. In Asian philosophy, this is the prana and the qi.

Reichenbach claimed that the Odic force is parallel to the electromagnetic field and its flux, but in the Odic force it's not opposite forces that attract, but like forces. Reichenbach tried to prove that sensitive people can see the colors of the Odic force and that they can willingly emanate its healing energy, especially from their palms, foreheads, and mouths. The force was named after god Odin who is known for his profound shamanic journey in the World Tree.

The electromagnetic field creates a flux of two opposing energies that ceaselessly spin from within and envelop the whole, uniting in the central vortex. The electromagnetic field resembles a torus as well as a tree with its branches and roots interconnected. In this sense, we could view our electromagnetic field and our life force as our Tree of Life. It's the ever-flowing field of vital energy and probably also the light body that connects us with all the realms in the World Tree of Life. Therefore, being conscious of our Tree of Life might be the key to activating our light body and its ability to venture through the axis mundi into the various interdimensional worlds.

Animals are known to be more connected to their heart centers than humans. They are able to detect the earth's electromagnetic field, which helps them with orientation and navigation in nature. In recent years, an intriguing scientific experiment has proven that humans have this ability as well, but it's underdeveloped. Our distant ancestors knew that animals and nature could be powerful guides if we opened our hearts and minds to their wisdom. In fairy tales and legends, heroes often prove their genuine compassion when they help animals, and that's why animals often reward them with supernatural gifts.

In the practice of kundalini yoga, the heart chakra is visually depicted as the *shatkona*, the hexagram made of two triangles. The triangle pointing upward stands for the masculine and the one pointing downward for the feminine, and their coalescence is the harmonious unity of these basic dualities, which have been regarded as the sacred marriage in hermetical and alchemical terminology.

The spine is where all the main energy centers called chakras are located. The chakras are revitalized by *nadi* channels through which the divine energy called prana flows. Three of the most important nadis are represented by a pillar, which is parallel to the spine, and two snakes that coil around it. The snakes rise from the base of the spine and meet again in the crown chakra, which has been depicted as a lotus or as wings. The snake also symbolizes the kundalini, a powerful energy that, when awakened, may lead to enlightenment.

Ancient depictions of the kundalini awakening resemble the caduceus, the staff of Hermes and Mercury. Kundalini also corresponds to the principles of the dualistic energy flow, and the central vortex of the torus and the electromagnetic field. Moreover, the two snakes and wings relate to serpent and bird symbolism in the World Tree of Life. And if we double the caduceus and mirror the two identical staffs, the resulting image begins to resemble the vortex of the torus or the electromagnetic field (see pictures on page 101).

In the human body, our spine could be parallel to the axis

mundi of our Tree of Life. The spine is symbolically the trunk, the staff, and the vortex of the toroidal electromagnetic field through which the two opposing energies travel. As they spiral from the center outward and then back to the center over and over, they energize our physical form and strengthen our connection with the worlds above and below, within and around us.

The heart of the axis mundi is the eternal here and now, the unity and oneness, the place of divine power and love. That's why, in Hindu philosophy, we become whole only once all the chakras and nadis are in balance. Then we are just as complete and self-sufficient as the torus. The seed is in all of us, waiting to develop into a wondrous Tree of Life that grows in harmony with the World Tree of Life.

There's another fascinating correlation between the axis mundi, the heart chakra shatkona, and the toroidal electromagnetic field. The underlying structure of the torus is the vector equilibrium (meaning symmetry of all vectors), which hides many symbols pertaining to the World Tree of Life such as crosses, rune Algiz, and the six-pointed star or the hexagram, therefore also the shatkona (see pictures). Furthermore, it conceals the double tetrahedron that is thought to be the core shape of the light body or the Merkaba.

Note: The core of the Merkaba being a double tetrahedron was brought forth by author and mystic Drunvalo Melchizedek in his book The Ancient Secret of the Flower of Life, volumes I and II.

Seed of Life and Flower of Life (from left to right).

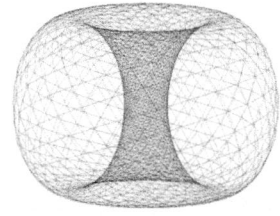

Celtic Tree of Life and torus (from left to right).

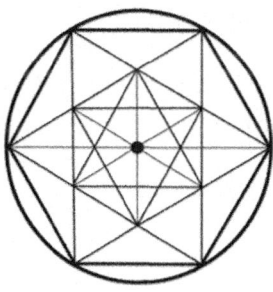
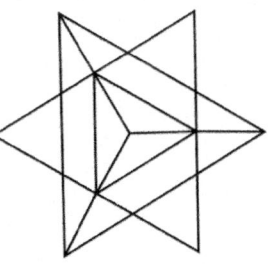

Vector equilibrium and double tetrahedron
aka Merkaba (from left to right).

The waves of the electromagnetic field that create the harmonious toroidal flow around the earth travel at the speed of light. This vibration could be seen as the earth's heartbeat, and it reverberates at certain frequencies known as Schumann resonances after the acclaimed physicist Winfried Otto Schumann. This earthly electromagnetic resonance has a rate that beats at 7.83 Hz, and the sound closest to it is no other than the spiritual sound *om* (pronounced *aummm*).

The earth vibrates at this frequency from the inside out, perpetually affecting all organisms on the planet. The rate has remained the same for thousands of years, but recent studies show that for some reason the frequency has been changing.

All these mystical connections imply that the most important core of our Tree of Life lies in the heart. Those who have had an out-of-body experience or who practice astral projection say that the heart center is the place via which the soul permeates the body and through which it leaves. Our heart is the key to the source of the central vortex of our electromagnetic field, or more symbolically, the seed from which the central trunk of our Tree of Life grows. Perhaps it is only once our heart begins to beat in tune with the heart of the World Tree of Life that we become a part of the joined, harmonious, ever-flowing and ever-expanding energy field.

The more aware we are of our own electromagnetic field, and therefore our Tree of Life, the more in tune we are with the World Tree of Life. The self-sustaining, self-revitalizing properties of the electromagnetic field of the earth hint at the possibility that our electromagnetic field could be just as powerful.

Furthermore, since the earth's electromagnetic field shields terrestrial life from ultraviolet radiation and ensures that life may thrive on its surface, our very own electromagnetic field could protect us from radiation and probably also from exposure to the electromagnetic smog caused by artificially generated electromagnetic fields in our environment. It is no coincidence that trees in particular have been proven to block these harmful electromagnetic fields. Even though our natural electromagnetic field may be disrupted by the artificial ones, the more we become aware of its extraordinary sustaining abilities, the more powerfully it shields us.

The following exercise is one of the ways to consciously align with this tremendous energy source:

The double helix in the Flower of Life.

Attuning to Our Tree of Life

This exercise is meant to make us more aware of our electromagnetic energy field, and therefore our Tree of Life. If performed regularly, it can help us remain conscious of the self-sustaining, self-revitalizing, and self-shielding life force we were all born with even though we may have lost touch with it throughout our lives. This exercise may also establish a better connection with our light body and its ability to travel through the various dimensions of reality in the World Tree of Life.

Important note: Please make sure you have read chapter two before doing this exercise. I don't claim that this exercise has a miraculous effect, but in my personal experience, tuning into my Tree of Life has proven very beneficial.

It's best to perform this exercise in a natural environment such as a forest, meadow, park, or a garden, but any calm space will do.

Start by relaxing in a comfortable standing position. The soles of your feet should be firmly on the ground and knees slightly bent for comfort. Now bring your attention to your heart, the seed of your Tree of Life. Slowly bring your palms together and let your fingertips touch so that they create a triangle pointing upward. This is the conscious, active part of the six-pointed star, which is the ancient symbol of the World Tree of Life and the heart chakra, as well as the underlying structure of the torus and the electromagnetic field of the heart.

Move your hands up toward your crown, then pull them apart and stretch them around your body and down toward your naval.

Once the palms meet again, let your fingertips touch so that they create a triangle pointing down, which represents the subconscious, passive part of the six-pointed star. Pull the triangle up your torso back to the heart and imagine the two triangles that you have metaphysically drawn merging into a complete six-pointed star.

The six-pointed star symbol represents the vector equilibrium or the core of the toroidal electromagnetic field, the light body also known as the Merkaba, and the heart chakra shatkona. Moreover, it is the most common ancient depiction of the World Tree of Life.

Imagine that the six-pointed star spreads out from your heart center and embraces your entire body. Now it turns into the torus, the electromagnetic field of your heart. Concentrate on the vortex of the torus that surrounds your torso. Visualize its spiraling energy flow that connects your feet and crown, expands into the wholeness of the torus, and returns within. Enjoy the energy flowing through you and around you, embracing your whole being in a harmonious energy field. It's a tree with its roots and branches interconnected. It's your Tree of Life. Visualize how your electromagnetic field flows in the same rhythm as the earth's electromagnetic field. Feel how your Tree of Life attunes to the World Tree of Life.

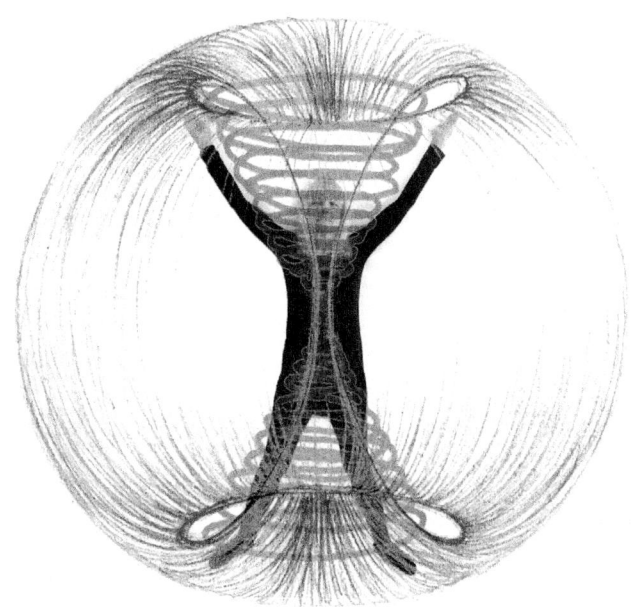

Bring your attention back to your center, the heart, and focus on how its beat matches the frequencies of the earth. Enjoy the harmonious exchange, feel how it invigorates and empowers you. Your Tree of Life and the World Tree of Life are one, now and always, flowing in the ceaseless energy fields of light and love.

Conclude the exercise with the following affirmation:

"I'm one with my eternal self-sustaining, self-revitalizing, and self-shielding tree of life, light, and love and in harmony with the eternal self-sustaining, self-revitalizing, and self-shielding World Tree of life, light, and love."

8

Tree Symbols, Signs, and Codes

In Paleolithic times, trees were mainly drawn as the shape that resembles the Old Germanic and Norse rune Algiz, also known as Elhaz, which is sometimes regarded as the bird's foot (the rune's name refers to the swan in Old Gothic but the elk in Old Germanic). Its common version represents a tree crown and the reversed version symbolizes tree roots (this became rune Yr in the Younger Futhark runes). Together, they make up various versions of the six-pointed star, which was profuse in ancient Slavic, Germanic, and Norse art. However, all the six-fold symbols relate to the prototypal pattern of creation known to Egyptian and Greek mystics as the Seed of Life that is the core of the Flower of Life. Sacred geometry, magical symbols, and runes can be seen as the codes that help us unveil the interconnectedness of everything and everyone in the World Tree of Life.

Most ancient depictions and descriptions of the World Tree of Life had animal guardians such as serpents, birds, or other winged beings. Moreover, they were often accompanied by spiked wheels called Sun Wheels or wheels of the year. Megalithic tombs in Brittany and Ireland depicted the Tree of Life on images of ships, which were viewed as celestial vehicles connecting the channel between this and the otherworldly realms. The trees on these ships were sometimes simplified into rods or staffs.

The main symbols for the Germanic and Norse World Tree were different variations of the six-pointed stars, also regarded as snowflakes. The idea was encompassed in the mother rune Hagal. The Younger Futhark version is depicted as a tree or a six-pointed star that contains all the other runes, and all the runes can also be derived from it. Another six-pointed rune similar to Hagalaz was the Anglo-Saxon rune Ior that represented the water serpent Jormungadr (see picture).

The Celtic Tree of Life has been depicted as a tree with its branches and roots entwined, which encapsulated the interconnectedness of the roots, trunk, and branches, and therefore also the past, present, and future as well as the netherworld, earth, and heaven. This tree symbol resembles the torus and the electromagnetic field (see chapter two). The underlying structure of the torus is the vector equilibrium that actually conceals various six-pointed stars and the double tetrahedron, which is thought to be the core of our light bodies, the Merkaba, as taught by mystic and author Drunvalo Melchizedek.

The tree symbols described in this chapter can be worked with during tree meditation, journeying, or ritual as they help us attune to the World Tree of Life, our own Tree of Life, and the harmonious connection between them. The tree symbols help us stimulate our multidimensional selves. Tree staffs especially inspire us to take hold of our divine power and understand that we are part of a greater world than we were taught at school, but more on that in the following chapter.

Common ancient World Tree of Life symbol.

Spiked wheels and cross/star symbols that represented the World Tree of Life in various ancient cultures.

Runes halag, ior, algiz/elhaz, and ír (from left to right).

Drawing the symbols, meditating with them, or visualizing them are all equally effective techniques. It's also beneficial to make a metaphysical tattoo (deciding on a certain symbol and visualizing or simply intending to imprint it on a preferred part of the body). Depending on our intention, we may decide to keep these metaphysical tattoos for protection, or as guidance from all the dimensions and realms of the World Tree of Life. We can keep them for as long as we like and can erase them just as easily as we created them – with a combination of intention and imagination.

All the following tree symbols meet in the complex symbolism of the World Tree of Life, and they all work together as a whole. That's why they are the keys to visualizing the incredible life force that flows within and around us.

The Celtic Tree of Life.

List of Tree Symbols

CROSS
The interconnectedness of worlds, dimensions, and timelines. The unity of the four basic elements including the fifth one that represents the center. Grounding/rooting as well as inner/outer growth.

SIX-POINTED STAR, HEXAGON, AND HEXAGRAM
Protection and shielding from all the realms, dimensions, and timelines in the World Tree of Life. The two-dimensional core of the light body and electromagnetic field. The blueprint of creation. Perfect symmetry.

EIGHT-POINTED STAR, OCTAGON, AND OCTAGRAM
The unity of the eight worldly directions. The eight pagan holidays. The eight realms of the World Tree of Life as viewed from the central one. Protection and shielding power from all the heavenly corners. The light body and the double tetrahedron, therefore, the three-dimensional six-pointed star, hexagon, and hexagram.

TRIANGLE
The basic trinity of trunk, roots, and branches. The three sacred springs at the roots of the Norse World Tree, Yggdrasil. The three tools (spinner, distaff, and spinning wheel) of the three Norns and Fates. The past, present, and future. Light, darkness, and shade. Life, death, and rebirth.

BIRD

The free, unattached, and unlimited spirit. A guide through the otherworldly realms. A symbol of spirit guides, extraterrestrials, and deities.

The trinity of life, death, and rebirth.

Water birds represent the connection between the earthly and celestial waters.

SERPENT

The wise guardian of divine knowledge, wisdom, and power. Natural cycles and renewal. The way out of the duality. The earthly and cosmic life force.

Self-revitalization and rejuvenation.

Like the bird, a guide through the otherworldly realms.

Note: It's important to differentiate between the malevolent and benevolent serpent of the World Tree of Life.

CIRCLE OR SPIKED WHEEL

The two-dimensional torus and the electromagnetic field.

The ever-changing cycles of life, death, and rebirth. The ceaseless changes, rejuvenation, and wheels of fortune.

The solar, lunar, and greater cosmic cycles.

PENTAGRAM

One of the basic patterns of creation.

Growth, development, movement, and cycles of life. The ceaseless motion in the electromagnetic field. Pentagram attunes us to the mystery of the "all in oneness" and the "one in the all."

STAFF, POLE, PILLAR, OR LADDER

Tree trunk and the vortex of the electromagnetic field. The axis mundi, and therefore the channel between the realms, dimensions, and timelines in the World Tree of Life. Human spine and the kundalini awakening. The power of the eternal here and now.

TORUS

The unity of all the tree symbols. Its underlying structure is the vector equilibrium, which contains triangles, crosses, six-pointed stars, eight-pointed stars, and pentagrams. It's also a three-dimensional circle and wheel. It represents the electromagnetic field and the light body, therefore, our Tree of Life and the World Tree of Life.
A completely harmonious, self-organizing, self-sustaining, and self-renewing energy flow.
The epitome of the World Tree of Life.

THE UNITY OF ALL THE TREE SYMBOLS

After Buddha reached enlightenment under the Bodhi Tree, he learned that to escape the wheels of karma, one should reach the center, the place from which everything derives and to which it returns. In a way, this is what the tree symbols teach us too, as all the geometric shapes arise either from a central point or a single line, which is its extension.

The single line mirrors the axis mundi and staff. The circle, sphere, and torus represent the electromagnetic field of the World Tree of Life, while the spirals and concentric circles symbolize its flow and cycles. The triangles, crosses, six-pointed stars, and eight-pointed stars are the underlying structure of the torus called the vector equilibrium (the symmetry of all vectors), and the spiked wheels are a two-dimensional, simplified depiction of the torus.

 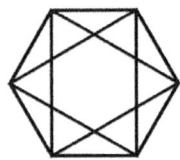 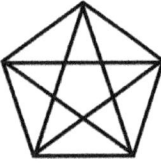

Octagon and octagram, hexagon and hexagram, pentagon and pentagram (from left to right).

Ogham

Besides tree symbols, there are also tree alphabets that function both as writing systems and as magical sets of codes. One of the most profound tree alphabets is the Celtic ogham where each sign represents an individual tree.

Some legends say that the ogham was a gift from Brigid, the goddess of poetry, arts, druidic wisdom, healing, sacred wells, and early spring. She's also the guardian of animals and the sacred, perpetually burning fire. Brigid's festival, Imbolc, shares her attributes of the serpent and swan, the two animals that also pertain to World Tree of Life symbolism. She's also often described as having two sisters or being a triple goddess.

Others claim that the ogham was brought to men by the Irish god of the written and spoken word, Ogma. Ogma is probably another name for the Celtic god Ogmios (British Ogmia) and could be the Celtic equivalent of the Germanic/Norse god of language and wisdom Wotan/Odin who legendarily taught the knowledge of the runes. Both Brigid and Ogma were children of Dagda, the father god and king of the legendary Irish deities Tuatha de Danann.

The oldest ogham inscriptions date back to the 5th and 6th centuries. The twenty signs were engraved in wood and stone either horizontally or diagonally and were mainly found in Ireland, Wales, and Scotland.

The Druids were believed to use these signs as a system of capturing their wisdom, philosophy, and teachings. They preferred ogham over the common writing system because, in their opinion, written words could be manipulated for political or religious agendas. Moreover, words could be easily misinterpreted and lose their true meaning in the hands of the uninitiated.

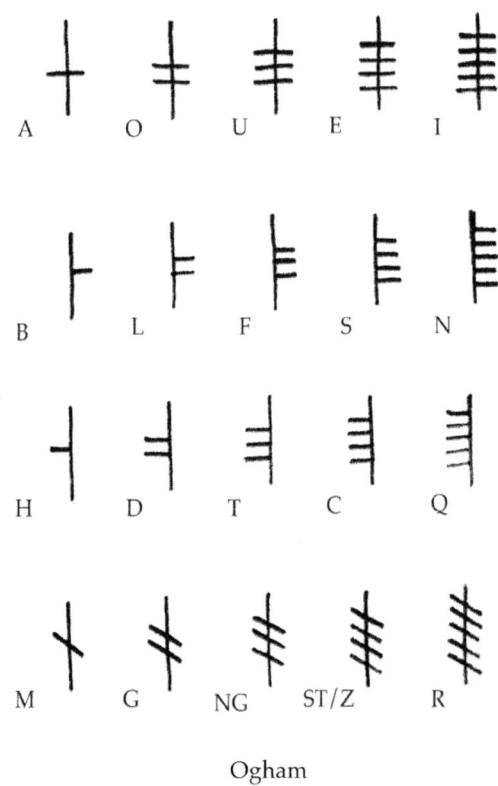

Ogham

The ogham was a clever set of secret codes that spoke only to those who were initiated in their mysticism. The ones who deciphered their symbolism received the tree wisdom and were able to work with it. That's why the Druids (both men and women) studied intensively for nine years before they could fully practice their tree magic and divination.

The wisdom of the Druids was suppressed during the 7th

century when the archbishop of Canterbury forbade gatherings and prayers at trees, stones, and wells. The church prelates must have known that these places were the gateways into otherworldly realms as churches, chapels, holy statues, and crosses were built on these ancient sites. Although some were meant to preserve these sacred thresholds, others intentionally blocked them. On top of that, fearful stories of hell were spread, scaring people away from the locations that led to the inner earth and the fairy mounds.

Once the netherworld had been shunned and our roots concealed, the main focus was given to the celestial realms. To this day, whatever is higher is considered more advanced and subsequently more spiritual than that which is lower. For centuries, roots and branches have been systematically separated and given different meanings, and the ancient wisdom of "as above, so below" or "as within, so without" became expressions of heresy. The Druids were right to be wary of the written word. Ancient wisdom was distorted in the new texts, philosophies, and laws.

Yet despite the religious manipulation and reorganization of society, some wise souls preserved the legacy of the ogham. In 14th century Ireland, the *Ogam Tract*, also called *The Book of Ogham* was written, capturing over one hundred variants of the ogham signs. A curious way of depicting the ogham was the Finn's Window, where the signs were arranged in concentric circles. This could be linked with the concentric spheres of the World Tree of Life and its axis mundi addressed in chapter two.

The name "Finn's Window" relates the Gaelic hero Finn or Fionn of the Fianna warriors who were believed to dwell in a cave, waiting to be summoned when Ireland needed their help. This correlates to the legend of the Bohemian Blanik knights who sleep inside the Blanik mountain and are to be awoken when they are needed the most. Since Bohemia was inhabited by Celts in the Iron Age, the two stories probably come from the same source. Interestingly, they also inspired J. R. R. Tolkien's characters of the Dead of Dunharrow in *The Lord of the Rings*.

The ogham consists of twenty main signs and five additional ones called Forfeda. Three of these resemble some of the Norse runes. The Koad could be compared with Gebo or Hagal, Uilleand to double Gebo, and Oir resembles rune Ingwaz or a distaff, which could be linked to the Norse Norns that mirror the triple goddess of the Celtic tradition.

Forfeda

The ogham was connected to the yearly sun cycles and also the moon cycles. The Celtic year had thirteen months that were shorter than the twelve we are accustomed to now, and each month was represented by a different tree.

The ogham helps us connect with the magical trees that were venerated by the ancient European tribes, especially by the Celts and their Druids. These people believed that the group spirits of the enchanted tree species, as well as the spirits of individual trees, could become wise guides to those who were conscious of them.

The ogham trees may guide us on the druidic path of tree magic, and some follow this path without even realizing it. The hedge and solitaire witches, wizards, and hermits all soak up the ancient wisdom of nature that has remained the same since the times when Merlin walked this earth.

A more concrete description of the ogham trees can be found in part three of this book, but here's a simple chart of the basic keywords:

B/Beith or Beithe/birch tree: The white lady of the woods, new beginning, revival and rejuvenation, health and vitality, motherly energy and protection, shielding against harmful energies, inner and outer harmony of light and shadow, beauty and grace, the purity of a spirit's divine essence.

L/Luis/originally meant flame or herb/rowan: Psychic protection and guidance, goddess of the land, motherly affection and care, the fire element, the pentagram and five-pointed star symbolism, overview, tree of hermits and hedge witches, freedom of spirit and creativity.

F/Fearn or Fern/alder: The elf king, the water element, intuition, psychic powers, emotional healing and emotional tests, emotional strength, subconscious and unconscious, making the unseen seen, third eye, connection to the elves, the ability to see beyond the veil of perception.

S/Saille/willow: The wise woman of the woods, the water element and the moon cycles, triple goddess, moon goddesses, intuition, psychic gifts, divination, enchantment, prophetic dreams.

N/Nuin, Nion, or Nin/originally meant lofty/ash: Sun energy and power, healing with light and solar power, inner strength, vitality and good health, connecting with the past, previous incarnations, ancestors, the World Tree of Life.

H/Huathe or Huath/hawthorn: The tree of lovers, sacred marriage, harmony between the subconscious and conscious mind, love and romance, emotional healing and empowering the heart center, affection, solicitude.

D/Duir/oak: The summer solstice, the king of the woods, fatherly protection and care, the sun and light, lightning and thunder, the doorway into other realms and dimensions, a powerful tree for journeying, inner power, strength and vitality, healing, deep peace, connection to the light half of the year and the Green Man archetype.

T/Tinne/originally meant iron pole/holly: The winter solstice, bringing issues from the subconscious to the light, balance of light and dark, connection to the Green Man archetype, protection against poisonous people, shielding from negativity and lightning strikes.

C/Coll/hazel: Magic, Communication, inspiration, divination, connection to the water and air elements, sacred knowledge and wisdom, connection to gods Mercury, Hermes, and Silvanus, a tree of artists especially poets and writers.

Q/Queirt or Quert, Ceirt or Cert/apple: Longevity or even immortality, inspiration, creativity, mind clarity, connection to the divine self and psychic abilities, the sacred symbols of the mandorla, vesica piscis, and the pentagram, the tree of the fairies, various goddesses, and the Sidhe, the tree of the Isle of Avalon that translates as "the isle of apple trees."

M/Muin/vine: Sun symbolism, warmth and light, the power of togetherness, provider of wisdom, knowledge and inspiration, harvest, abundance, creativity, peaceful mind and soul, visions and inspiration.

G/Gort/this ogham originally meant field/ivy: Determination, hardiness, persistence, free-minded and goal-driven souls, wanderers, travelers, journeys and cycles. Together with vine it represents the DNA spiral and pertains to the spiral and serpent symbolism.

NG/NGéadal or Gétal/original meaning of the word is unknown/broom or reed: Magical act of sweeping, cleansing the outer and inner space, energy cleansing of the home.

Neopagan tradition recognizes this ogham as reed, which is also linked with cleansing, particularly on an emotional level.

Z/Straif or Straiph/originally probably meant sulfur and therefore could have an alchemical connotation/blackthorn: Protection against evil, shielding from curses and negativity, strength and resilience, life's polarities: dark and light, yin and yang, action and reaction.

R/Ruis/originally meant reddening/elder: Another tree pertaining to goddess symbolism, fairies, Sidhe, elves, natural deities. Appeases fear, offers psychic protection, shields from all negative intrusions.

A/Ailm/original meaning of the word is uncertain/fir and possibly elm:

Fir: Protection from curses or sorcery, repels negativity and dark moods, renewing qualities of nature, symbolism of pinecones therefore also third eye and its ability to see into the otherworldly realms.

Elm: Healing, rejuvenation, rebirth, connection to roots, kin and ancestors, subterranean realms, the worlds of the Sidhe.

O/Onn or Ohn/originally meant ash tree/gorse or furze: The sun and fire element, abundance, hardiness, dualities of creativity and destruction that result in purification.

U/Úr/originally meant moisture or soil/heather: Love and romance, connection with the otherworldly realms and dimensions, calming and soothing, rejuvenating and healing. (There's an interesting parallel to the Norse rune Uruz, which is, too, associated with healing and the water element.)

E/Eadhadh, Edad, or Eadha/original meaning of the word is unknown/aspen or white poplar: Both trees have a shielding and healing power, connect with the air element and air elementals, help us channel the gods of communication such as Hermes, Mercury, or Odin, and attract powerful visions. Moreover, both trees have been known to have entrances to the fairy and Sidhe realms.

I/Iodhadh, Idad, Idhadh, or Ioho/original meaning of the word is unknown/yew: The World Tree of Life, self-sustaining and self-restoring quality of the torus and the electromagnetic fields, shielding, hardiness and endurance, renewal and energetic healing, rejuvenation, new paths and levels of awareness, the ever-changing changelessness.

Runes

While the ogham helps us tune in to the wisdom of individual, enchanted tree species, the runes are the sacred symbols of creation inherently connected with the World Tree of Life. In Norse mythology, runes are carved into the Yggdrasil by the Norns, the three giantesses who spin the fate of the nine realms. The legend of how the runes came to men, however, ties in to god Odin. According to legend, Odin received the knowledge of the runes during a shamanic journey into the roots of the Yggdrasil. There, in the well of ancestral wisdom, he perceived the magical meaning and power of the signs and shared them with his fellow Aesir gods as well as humankind.

The runes remain mystical, archetypal, and free. They are interpreted in various ways depending on the intuition and creativity of a given mind, but their symbolism is based on the medieval Icelandic, Norwegian, and Anglo-Saxon rune poems.

There are two most common sets of runic alphabets: The Elder Futhark consists of the twenty-four oldest runes that are, along with an extra nine, also part of the Anglo-Saxon alphabet. The Younger Futhark contains only sixteen runes from the original Elder Futhark, though some of them differ in depiction and symbolism from the original set.

Each rune is a profound symbol in the Yggdrasil's mystery, and together they represent a mystical alphabet of nature. All the runes pertain to some part of the World Tree of Life; however, some of them have been used as tree symbols even in other parts of the world. These were mainly Algiz, Tiwaz, and the Younger Futhark version of Hagalaz called Hagal. Working with the runes opens our consciousness to the World Tree of Life and our own multidimensional being, our Tree of Life.

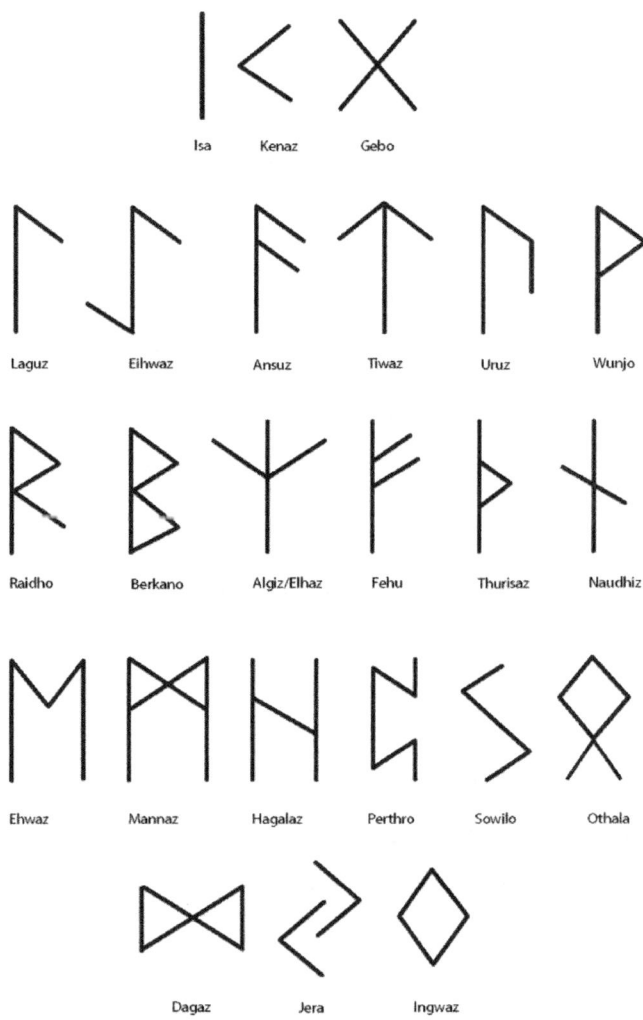

Runes give us divination and manifestation that complement natural magic, affirmation, and alchemy. Once we attune to their wisdom, we may work with them like the other tree symbols. We can visualize them, draw them, meditate on them, do a metaphysical tattoo, or invite them on a shamanic tree journey. We may also chant them or perform runic postures (more in my book *Runes: Magical Codes of Nature*).

Here is a simple list of the oldest and most widely used set of runes, the Elder Futhark:

I/Isa/means icicle: The power of ice, stillness, centering, meditation, inner world, inward processes, waiting before acting, thinking things through.

K and C/Kenaz/means torch: The power of fire, torch, fire in human hands, creativity, passion and drive, following heart's desire, life's purpose, light and warmth.

G/Gebo/means gift: Gifts from the gods, harmony between dualities, masculine and feminine, sacred marriage, the god and the goddess unity, psychic protection, the strength of saying no or blocking situations we do not resonate with.

D/Dagaz/means day: The daily cycles, day and night, light and dark, warmth and cold, focus on daily activities, contemporary events and insights.

J/Jera/means year or harvest: The yearly cycles, harvest, abundance, the light and dark halves of the year, you reap what you sow.

S/Sowilo/means sun: The sun, inner strength, divine self, power to create and destroy, wise approach to personal power, manifestation and magic yet bearing in mind the "what comes around goes around" effect.

L/Laguz/means leek and water: The water element, emotions and feelings, intuition and deep insights, dreams and visions, inner processes, psychic gifts, subconscious and unconscious.

P/Perthro/means device for fortune telling: Destiny versus free will, the wheels of time, cleansing karmic issues or events, forgiveness, anything to do with divination and magic, greater cycles of life in the World Tree of Life.

U/Uruz/means drizzle or aurochs: Healing power of the water and earth elements, mother goddess, strength and endurance, vitality and good health.

TH/ Thurisaz /means thorn: The ability to stand one's ground, protection against enemies, shielding from detrimental forces, personal will.

T/Tiwaz/means god Tiwaz or Tyr: Inner hero or heroine, the power to decide and be in charge of one's life, free will versus justice and balance, courage and drive, the ability to speak one's truth, symbolically also the World Pillar of the Irminsul and therefore the axis mundi.

B/Berkano/means birch tree: Renewal, cleansing, a new phase or a new beginning, purity, healing power of Mother Earth, protection.

R/Raidho/means chariot or wagon: The wheels of fortune, change, progress, cycles in life, traveling, shamanic journeys, moving on from something or someone.

V and W/Vend and Wunjo/means joy: Freyr and Freya, nature deities, animal guides, inner child, happiness and joy, the here and now, enjoying every moment, gatherings and reunions, good relation with others, thankfulness, blessings.

N/Naudhiz/means need: Represents whatever we are in need of and helps us see the necessity of focusing on the important things.

E/Ehwaz/means horse: Odin's horse, the light body aka Merkaba, a good bond, shamanic journeys, freedom, great assets (mainly spiritual ones).

M/Mannaz/means human: Mankind, being humane, divine potential of humans, ancestors, gods and men, power of humanity, individual versus society.

F/Fehu/means cattle and money: Money and wealth, owning versus being owned, well-paid work, property and assets, abundance on all the levels of existence.

A/Ansuz/means ancestral god and divinity: The divine self, the divine heritage, ancestral guidance and wisdom, spirit guides, metaphysical guidance.

Ei/Eihwaz/means yew tree: Hardiness and strength, endurance, togetherness, importance of sticking together, the trinity of life, death, and rebirth, interdimensional traveling, a gateway into the other realms, the World Tree of Life.

Z/Algiz and Elhaz/means swan (Algiz) and elk (Elhaz): The earthly and celestial realms, tree branches and roots, spiritual expansion and growth, divine protection and shielding.

O/Othala/means property and home: Earthly as well as otherworldly homes, home is where the heart is, family and kinship, safety, good base, stability, ancestral spirit guides.

Ing/Ingwaz/means god Ing (Freyr): God Freyr and his sister Freya, nature deities, the gateways into the other realms and dimensions, deep concentration or meditation, breakthrough, threshold.

H/Hagalaz/means hail or egg: The primordial pattern of existence, the cosmic egg, the unity of all the runes. The younger version is depicted as one of the most common symbols of the World Tree of Life and makes a powerful symbol of protection.

The runes and ogham are innately present in nature, and once our consciousness opens up to their guidance, we start taking heed of them. Both the runic and ogham signs can be spotted in trees and tree branches but also in grass, straw, random wooden sticks, or stones. Each of the codes and their combinations deliver unique messages. Once they begin to pop up on our path during walks in nature, we can be certain that we are on the right path to understanding tree magic. The wisdom of the most archetypal language of all – the language of nature – then begins to speak to us and through us, waking us to the ancient knowledge we all once had.

Here are some examples of the ogham and runes in nature:

9

WORKING WITH MAGIC STAFFS AND WANDS

In the first part of this book, we learned that countless ancient deities, heroes, and saints were depicted with staffs that shared similar attributes. Since staffs were one of the first magical objects banned during the strict Catholic Christianization period in the Middle Ages, it proves just how powerful they must have been in the eyes of the ancients. Staffs belonged to the Druids, hermits, prophets, shamans, and sages who were aware of their divine power and were in tune with their own Tree of Life as well as the World Tree of Life.

The magic staff is an intermediary between the inner and outer worlds – a shield – and if the spirit of the original tree joins, then it can even be a spirit guide. In this sense, the purpose of the magic staff is to provide a channel between our own magical powers and those of the multiverse. When we find the right magic staff, it becomes a friend for life. It is enough to simply hold it for support to instantly feel its vibrant tree energy.

A wand is a smaller version of a staff. Magic wands have been used as tree amulets and talismans because they are easier to carry around. They are also ideal when casting a magic circle or metaphysically drawing symbols and runes over someone or something.

Finding Your Magic Staff or Wand and Making First Contact

Finding your magic staff is a truly festive moment that brings together the powerful trinity of your Tree of Life, the spirit of the tree that the branch came from, and the World Tree of Life. From my experience, once you have begun to long for your magic staff, it will soon cross your path.

The staff usually comes from a tree that you already know and enjoy spending time near to. It's best to avoid cutting off a living branch or killing a young sapling for a staff, as some ignorant people do, because the tree spirit could then cut ties with you in return. This is quite understandable as nobody likes to befriend someone who hurt them or took something from them without asking. If you have already done so and have apologized for it, you may be able to develop a bond with the tree and its branch regardless, depending on how fond the tree spirit is of you. However, if you do cut off a living branch, it should be one that is calling out to you or seems to be ready to break off anyway. I personally prefer to wait for the tree to give me its branch, and this often happens after a strong wind or a thunderstorm during which branches break off naturally. Finding a recently fallen branch that is still vital signifies that you have received a great gift from the tree.

Once you set out on the path of tree magic, you will probably attract various magic staffs and wands, each of which will represent a different part and mission of your Tree of Life in the World Tree of Life. To welcome the wisdom of the individual staff and its mother tree into your life, make contact by holding it, observing its shape, and trying to tune in to its energy field. Insights and ideas will permeate your mind. It's important to note down the first impressions you have about the staff as these will never be repeated.

After you have established a good connection with your staff, ask it what its purpose is in your life, and open your mind to receiving intuitive thoughts, impressions, or symbols. Some staffs and wands can be quite chatty, while others take time to express themselves. The most powerful initiation into the magic of your new staff is, however, the moment when you take it with you for a walk or inner journey.

If you don't feel any connection to your staff despite your best efforts, try asking it for an explanation when you take it for a walk. Then you might begin to see some tree symbols, runes, or ogham on your path and put the messages together like a mosaic (see previous chapter for more information on the tree symbols). Some staffs take longer to tune in to than others. Always treat the staff with respect, though, and thank it for being with you on your magical path. Treat it as a friend, not a tool, as only then can you make that special connection. If the staff is still not communicating, give it some more time and let it soak up the atmosphere of your energy field. Some staffs prefer to simply be the guardians of your space and should not be worked with magically. They may be content to decorate your home and shield it from negativity.

If the staff feels alien to you even after you have tried to establish a connection, or if its wood shows signs of disease, it's probably not your lifelong staff companion after all. In that case, thank it for the time you have spent together and for the purpose it came with, and take it back to its place of origin or to a calm forest, park, or meadow – any place where it can become one with nature again.

Finding a magic wand is much easier than a staff as it is smaller. Wands are also more practical because we can easily carry them around. A wand from a tree root follows the inner spiral of the past, the inner earth, or other earthly dimensions. A wand from a tree branch, on the other hand, symbolically guides us on the outward spiral to the future and celestial realms. A wand with a serpentine shape fortifies our bond with earthly energies or may represent the serpent guardian of our Tree of Life.

Based on what information you have received during your first mindful connection with your staff or wand, you should become more aware of what magical purpose it has on your path. It may be an empowering one, a meditative one, a journeying one, a protective one, a purging one, an inspiring one, and so forth.

Preparing Your Magic Staff and Caring for It

Before you and your staff set out on a magical path together, it's crucial to make sure its wood is healthy and strong. Let me share a few tricks that I have learned from my friend Eric who works with wood for creative and magical purposes.

First, do a simple test to see if the staff you have found is in good shape. If the branch bounces back or remains straight when you slightly bend it, it means that it's still vital. However, if it begins to break off, it's already decaying. If you peel off its bark and see that there's a fresh, green layer underneath (the cambium layer), it means that the wood is healthy and can be further worked with.

The next step is to prepare the staff and keep caring for it so that your journey together is long and fruitful. It's best to scrape the bark off, as this is prone to fungi and other bacteria. Once the branch is separated from its tree, there's no life in it anymore, and so you don't have to worry about hurting it. On some branches, the upper layer is very thin and not easy to get rid of, which means that the branch should be kept the way it is or just treated with some sandpaper. It's best to learn more about the tree that the staff came from and find out how to properly care for its wood.

The next step is to leave the staff in a dry, gently heated, or cool place that has a good source of fresh air. It's important to avoid moisture and keep it away from direct heat. The wood needs to dry slowly, so it's best to let it rest for a few weeks. You will intuitively know the right time to continue working on it.

When the staff feels dry, you may want to slightly polish the rough edges with sandpaper and apply a protective layer of linseed, walnut, or olive oil. It's good to oil the wood at least three times before using it. Depending on the wood, some staffs may need to be varnished in order to complete the preparation while others like to keep a purely natural look, but you will sense what your magic companion needs.

As for caring for the staff continually, some staffs will benefit from being in the fresh air from time to time or from imbibing sunshine or moonshine. Avoid leaving the wood in damp or stuffy places, though, because these tend to attract fungi. During a contemplation, meditation, or an inner journey, you will find out more about how your staff likes to be recharged. While some staffs react well when you take them for walks, others prefer to be your journey guides or home guardians. Some staffs may even keep guard by your bed and guide you in dreams.

Moreover, your staff will appreciate being oiled each time it has used up a lot of energy or if it has been for a long hike with you. You will intuit what it needs in order to stay strong or which oil to use as a protective layer. Sometimes you may want to add some essential oils to the carrier oil for specific purposes. If you sense that the staff needs to be energized or rejuvenated, try mint, lemon balm, verbena, or various citrus scents. If the staff asks for grounding, it's best to use earthly oils such as cinnamon, cedar, or frankincense. And if it needs to be cleansed of negative energy or trauma, try sage, thyme, rosemary, or lavender. Staffs react especially well when you apply oils that you have made yourself from plants, which have been harvested with respect and gratitude.

Once you learn more about your staff, you may want to decorate it with some appropriate carved or painted magical symbols, runes, ogham, and so forth. It's also wonderful to embed the wood with some crystals or wrap a string of beads or feathers around it. As for the feathers, though, try finding them yourself in nature and avoid using shop-bought feathers; you don't know where they have come from and how the animal was treated. All the objects and symbols that you decorate your staff with should have a deep meaning to you and represent the purpose that the staff has in your life. Besides caring for the staff physically, it's important to align with its energy by appreciating it, contemplating and meditating with it, or taking it for walks in wild, natural environments.

It's important to keep in mind that the staff is a fragment of its tree and therefore preserves the character of its origin. That's why it's so powerful to have a staff from a tree that you have already established a connection with. Depending on how strong your bond is with the mother tree, its spirit may visit the staff or become one of your spirit guides. Either way, it's good to bring the staff to its mother tree from time to time, especially if it's near your home. Most staffs recharge and become more powerful close to their roots. In the words of the poet Francois Villon, "all things to one tend to seek the place of their origins," and your staff is no exception.

The group spirit of the tree species that your magic staff came from will tell you a lot about its magical and healing properties, and that's why it's good to pay attention to its legacy. The symbolism of individual trees can be found in part three of this book.

The same care applies to magic wands.

Welcoming the Power of the Elements into Your Staff

Recharging your magic staff in sunlight and moonlight invites the elements of light and fire into its energy field, but there are other elements to welcome into its wood and thus empower it for your magical journey together.

The basic elements in some ancient cultures were simply water and fire (or ice and fire in Norse mythology), but most agree that the classical elements are air, water, fire, and earth, plus metal in Asian cultures. The all-permeating and unifying element called ether has unfortunately been disregarded throughout modern history because it is explainable and understandable only to the spirit, not the senses. Yet it's the ether that permeates all the elements and unifies them into a complete masterpiece. Ether is the center as well as the whole. Trees react to all the elements and cycles of nature yet remain standing in their power center no matter what, and this quality applies to the tree staffs as well.

In order to invite all the elements into your tree staff and therefore enhance its magical power, it's enough to consciously ask the element to bless your shared path.

To charge your staff with the grounding earth element, which attracts endurance and vitality, take a walk with your magic staff or simply stand with it on the ground somewhere in a calm, natural environment.

To invite the invigorating fire element that brings inspiration, passion, and creativity, it's best to let your magic staff soak up some sunlight and starlight.

To attract the nourishing water element, which is our guide through the inner worlds and a boost to our intuition and psychic abilities, it's best to bring your magic staff to a natural body of water or hold it above an underground spring and let its vibrant energy infuse the wood. You may even feel guided to dip the staff in water, but don't leave it there for more than a few seconds so it does not become susceptible to mildew.

And, finally, to unite your magic staff with the refreshing air element, which inspires communication and mental activity, try gently waving or shaking it in the air. This is especially powerful when you are in the fresh air.

The ether is innately present in your magic staff and can be felt when you focus on your connection with it. The key to the fifth element is in your heart, so the fonder you are of your staff, the more powerful the fifth element becomes.

If you take your magic staff for a walk, you begin to feel how all the elements communicate with it. It is in movement that staffs attract the magical energy of the elementals, the spirits of various elements, and thus help us connect with them and channel their wisdom. The more often you spend time with your staff in nature, the more vibrant and harmonized it becomes. In time, you may experience just how powerful a mediator your staff is, but in the words of the Druids, "this path needs to be discovered individually and remain your own."

Magical Workings with Staffs and Wands

Since trees, staffs, and wands are physical representations of the World Tree of Life, they can be seen as the channels between our Tree of Life and the World Tree of Life.

With a tree staff or wand, it's easier to be centered and grounded in our divine power source. Moreover, our magic tree companions help us tune in to the dimensions and realms that exist simultaneously with ours. That's why it's good to hold your magic staff or wand during deep meditations, channeling, inner journeying, and astral travel, or to place it by your bed before you go to sleep.

Staffs and wands have an empowering quality. Whenever you feel dispirited or lack energy, it's enough to hold your magic staff or wand and enjoy the abundant flow of revitalizing energy. A staff in particular can also become the powerful weapon of a spirit warrior. The spirit warrior has often been misunderstood and associated with war in a physical sense. The spirit warrior, however, doesn't thrive on aggression; it thrives on assertiveness. We awaken the spirit warrior when we need to stand our ground or protect ourselves and our loved ones. It helps us avoid harm and casts away negativity. Some shamans hold on to their staffs as a protection before or during an inner journey, and even use them to banish demonic entities. A fully charged and revered tree staff protects us from negativity. It's enough to consciously stand in our power and hold on to the staff, and all evil is instantly repelled. Just remember what Gandalf achieved with his staff in *The Lord of the Rings*, as he's a unique character who portrays the wisdom of the Druids and shamans.

Whenever we practice magic or work with the power of manifestation, it's essential to ensure we remain on the path of light, not darkness, as we know that what comes around goes around. Therefore:

Never go against someone else's free will.
Only wish for things that are for the benefit of everyone involved.
Be aware of the cause and effect or action and reaction of all, not only magical, actions.

If you treat your magic staffs and wands well and appreciate them, they will become your lifelong companions who will help you rediscover your multidimensional, divine self and your inherent magical powers.

10

Tree Meditations, Journeying, and Rituals

In this chapter, I'm going to draw from my personal experiences, but I strongly encourage you to create your own tree meditations and rituals, as each person has a unique inner guidance when it comes to tree magic.

Runic Tree Meditation

This is a simple standing meditation that helps us tune in to the runes pertaining to the World Tree of Life. It also energizes us, empowers us, and shields us from negative forces. It's best performed in a natural environment such as a forest, meadow, park, or garden, but standing in a comfortable indoor space with your bare feet on the floor will do. All the runes can be exercised as magical postures that help us draw in their profound magic. (More in my book *Runes: Magical Codes of Nature*.)

The starting position aligns us with our Tree of Life's trunk. Stand in a basic posture with your feet close together. Raise your hands above your head so that your body resembles a straight line. This is the first runic posture of Isa, the rune of stillness, concentration, and the eternal here and now. Focus on your heart and pronounce Isa (read *isa* as in *Lisa*).

Next, lift your hands up and spread them apart as if you'd like to embrace the sky. This is the second runic posture of Algiz, the classic symbol for trees and a rune of our divine selves and connection to the celestial realms and spirit guides. Imagine that your hands are like tree branches, absorbing energy from the sky. You may feel like slightly shaking your palms and fingers as you enjoy the energy flow. Pronounce Algiz (read *al* as in *alas* and *giz* as in *Giza*).

Finally, drop your hands down so that they slant not far from your hips. This is the third runic posture of Tiwaz, the rune of the World Pillar called Irminsul as well as the rune of the spirit warrior, inner power, and balance. Focus your attention on the earth, your spirit's home, as well as your inner strength. Imagine that your hands are soaking up the earth energy and that your feet are rooted in the ground. If you feel like it, slightly shake your palms and fingers to emphasize the energy flow. Pronounce Tiwaz (read *ti* as in *tin* and *waz* as in *was*).

Now return to the starting position, but leave your hands by your hips to achieve another version of the Isa runic posture. Focus on your Tree of Life and its expansion and growth in the World Tree of Life. Notice how by performing these runic stances you draw the snowflake or six-pointed star around your body, which is the ancient symbol of the World Tree of Life, the unity of all existence, and the divine light.

Making a Tree Friend

To find a tree that resonates with you is like finding a good friend. First, you need to feel the initial click and then, as you establish the connection, you may develop a long-lasting companionship.

If your heart is open to trees and tree elementals, you will intuitively know when you find a tree being whose spirit speaks to you. Then you may learn more about each other and decide whether you have the potential to become friends. Simply spending some time in the tree's presence is enough, and there is no need to rush anything. Trees usually prefer to be approached from a distance at first, and just like anyone, they like to be appreciated and hear a compliment every now and then. The more you admire the tree, the more likely it is that it will open up to you.

One thing that should be mentioned is that trees see right into our hearts and recognize the intention we approach them with. If it's a selfish intention and we just want the tree to help us with something without making any effort ourselves or giving anything in return, the tree will probably sever the connection or not even start it in the first place.

That being said, it's good to start the relationship by doing something nice for the tree. Perhaps you could move some trash from its vicinity or bring it a gift such as a nice stone or other natural object and place it on the ground somewhere only you know.

With time, the tree may become your confidant and you will probably feel a flow of inspiration and wisdom in its presence. For example, you could receive an immediate answer to something you have been wondering about or experience a sudden breakthrough.

You might even sense its spirit nearby. Trees like it when we are calm, especially in our minds that are usually so busy with thoughts. Meditating by the tree or just daydreaming is a wonderful start, and who knows, maybe the tree will become your journey tree as well (see Tree Journeying).

Relaxing nearby and paying attention to how you tend to feel or think around the tree opens your heart and mind to its unique spirit. To feel connected to your tree friend even when you are not in its presence, you may take something from it as a reminder of your bond. Perhaps a branch that has recently broken off and is still vital, or some of the local soil and stones. Also, depending on the tree species and the season, you might like to take a seed, nut, fruit, or leaf that you like and that the tree would eventually shed anyway.

It's common to suddenly feel the desire to hum or sing in the presence of your tree friend because tree elementals love music, especially that which comes straight from your heart. They also love poetry and stories. In fact, many trees function as a kind of natural memory disk and store local stories and wisdom. With time, your tree friend may even start sharing some stories with you, or perhaps you will feel drawn to tell it your own story. Then, your tree friend might preserve your message and wisdom for the next generation of seekers who may also find comfort between its roots and crown.

Planting a Guardian Tree

In ancient times, people planted guardian trees near their homes or in the center of their settlements. The tree became a part of their family or society and was honored as a wise being that one could contemplate next to and receive guidance from. This tradition has died out, but in some parts of the world it's still remembered. In many old European villages, we still find such guardian trees, and although people may not venerate them as they used to, the locals still enjoy the wayside shrines, benches, or resting spots near to them. The most common European guardian trees were oaks, beeches, lindens, walnuts, chestnuts, or olive trees.

Planting a guardian tree is a beautiful ritual. If you don't have the option to plant one near your home, you can do it at your favorite spot in a forest, park, or any place that you frequently visit and that you know will be safe and beneficial for the tree.

Sometimes, when you decide to plant a guardian tree in a special location, you may find one that actually wants to be replanted. It may be a small sapling or a damaged tree that is calling out for help because it's not doing so well in its current location. Always make sure the tree roots come out easily, though, and dig carefully around it to take as many roots as possible. I have found three trees this way. One was a recently fallen young maple whose roots were already exposed above the soil, and the second and third were birch and ash saplings that were too close to the road and ready to relocate. Amazingly, they came out easily as I gently pulled them up, and there was no need for digging.

For some guardian trees, however, it's best to simply go to a gardening shop and choose a tree that calls out to you. The intention of purchasing a guardian tree is enough to start the magical ritual. Timing is important too. If you find your guardian tree by chance then it doesn't matter, but if you can make a plan, then choose autumn or spring, shortly after the full moon, and in the evening, as the roots are most active during those times. To make a stronger bond with the tree, add a part of your own DNA to its roots before you pour in water and cover them with soil – this may be some hair, nail clippings, or a drop of spit. This makes sure that the tree aligns with your energy field and becomes your guardian. Then welcome the spirit of the tree by giving it a gift that means something to you such as a stone, a crystal, another natural object, or a glass of good wine, but don't overdo this as you wouldn't want your guardian tree to get drunk, would you?

To conclude the ritual, welcome the tree into its new environment, promise to be its guardian, and ask it to be yours in return. Henceforth, it's important to take good care of your tree, provide it with water, nutrients, and some kind words here and there. If the tree continues to feel appreciated and loved, it will be your tree friend for life.

Tree Journeying

This kind of journeying is ideal when you need to receive an answer to a question or simply seek guidance in your inner worlds. I learned this method from my friend, a visionary author and mystic, Ayn Cates Sullivan, but put my own spin on it. Ayn taught me how to journey with trees when I took her to my favorite linden grove. I have always felt that the lindens are powerful guardians of the area and that they conceal many secret thresholds into the otherworldly realms, but Ayn made me aware of how I can journey past these thresholds. About six months later, after a windy storm, I found four fallen branches by the lindens and these became my magic staffs. With time, I learned that each of them has a different purpose and one of them is actually my journey staff. For Ayn's method, you don't need a journey staff, but if you have one, then it's only natural to hold it for grounding, guidance, and protection each time you set out on that inner adventure. You may also choose to hold a wand or other talisman from your journey tree; just follow whatever feels right.

Before you journey, pick a tree friend that you already feel in tune with or one that you sense guards a threshold into a realm that resonates with you. Once you feel that the right time has come and your soul calls out for guidance from an otherworldly realm, choose a place where you will be undisturbed and prepare yourself for your inner tree journey.

First, try to relax your body and mind and find a comfortable position. Avoid lying down if you tend to fall asleep during meditations. I strongly recommend that you imagine a protective symbol or call upon your spirit guides, asking to be shielded and made safe during the journey, and only visit the places that are in tune with you and are meant to deliver messages for your greatest good. You can listen to a recording of the monotonous sound of shamanic drums or ask someone you trust to drum for you if possible.

When you feel relaxed and your mind is completely calm, focus on the tree you choose to journey with and on its vicinity. Imagine yourself standing by it, and state the reason why you wish to journey, as now is the time to specify what your intention is.

When you feel ready, look for a portal. You will intuitively know where the portal is. It may open up in the trunk, the roots, or branches, but there may also be a portal somewhere in the tree's vicinity. It could be an underground portal or a sky portal, but try to not block yourself by assuming that the sky is energetically cleaner than the earth. Just remember that you are shielded by your Tree of Life as you journey and that there is no higher or lower realm. The below reflects in the above and the above in the below, the within communicates with the without and vice versa. And if you are protected by your spirit guides and the tree symbols, you don't have to fear any heavy inner realms.

Once you find the portal, enter it. You should now start to experience something. Either you will feel as if you have just crossed over to somewhere or you will begin to descend or ascend. The speed and time spent on the journey should feel natural. After you reach the place you are meant to visit, your own private journey ensues. You may meet the spirit of the tree you are journeying with, a deceased loved one, some of your spirit guides, guardian animals, ancestors, or a deity you venerate. Perhaps you will go to your home realm or another timeline for guidance; it all depends on your divine self and where it takes you…

When you feel ready to journey back, seek out the portal again. It might appear in a different place than before, but by crossing it or descending or ascending through it, you will return to your current time and space. I recommend noting down everything you have experienced including the details you may deem unnecessary as every part of the whole has a deep meaning. The guidance or messages often manifest in riddles, symbols, or synchronicity, and these might make more sense later. Moreover, they need to be deciphered by no one but yourself.

For me personally, it's best to journey in darkness, especially at night as that's when the inner light switches on better. However, since each person is different, you may have a different experience altogether. I also encourage you to put your own spin on the tree journeying, which will be completely in tune with your own Tree of Life.

Attuning to the Bird and Serpent Guardians of Your Tree of Life

In mythology, legend, and various religions all over the world, birds have symbolized the spirit, the soul, and interdimensional journeying. For example, water birds such as the swan or duck were ridden by various deities to demonstrate their journeys between the earthly and celestial waters that reflect in one another and are reminiscent of the hermetical "as above, so below." Doves have always symbolized guidance from spirit guides while crows brought messages from the ancestors. The bird guardians of the World Tree of Life are easier to connect with as their spiritual purpose has not been tainted with misapprehension like the purpose of the serpentine guardians.

The serpent is mainly connected to the earth, vitality, and rejuvenation. It also represents the self-sustainable energy of the electromagnetic field and the kundalini. The wise serpent guardian of the World Tree of Life has been misunderstood because some demonic beings resemble reptiles, serpents, worms, or spiders (more in chapter five). While the benevolent serpents represent the healing power of the earth, wisdom, and enlightenment, the demonic ones aspire to lead the initiate astray (though they may pose as helpers at first). In this sense, I would like to quote well-known Czech mystic and author Hana Sar Blochova who once told me: "It's important to differentiate between the benevolent and malevolent reptilians and serpentine beings in this dualistic reality."

It takes some experience and knowledge of the various realms and beings to be able to tell them apart, but there's one simple piece of advice that almost always applies: Whenever something or someone stirs up fear or hate, causes you to doubt yourself or, on the contrary, makes you feel superior, it's not a benevolent entity.

To attune to the bird and serpent of your own unique Tree of Life, it's good to do an inner journey (see Tree Journeying) with the intention of meeting the two archetypal guardians. There are probably many more animal spirit guides that you are meant to meet on your inner journeys, but these two have proven to be crucial in sustaining the harmony of the Tree of Life. Sometimes they both appear during the same journey; other times, it takes more journeys to learn more about them.

After the journey, pay attention to synchronicity. You might even meet snakes or birds on your path or be drawn to their mythical counterparts. Once you become fully conscious of them, they will guide you to the greater knowledge of your Tree of Life and the World Tree of Life. You can always seek their advice or journey with them. Sometimes they may ask something of you in return, but as mentioned before, your true spirit guides and guardians never ask for anything that causes you to doubt yourself or that stirs fear, hate, superiority, or selfishness.

Although there is no difference between the above and below, it's common for the bird guides to take us to the celestial realms and the various dimensions of the universe while the serpent guides show us around the various dimensions of the earth.

Furthermore, the bird of your Tree of Life will teach you how to feel unlimited and free. It will assist you with your psychic abilities and might even teach you how to fly in your inner realms. The serpent of your Tree of Life will teach you about your own revitalizing, rejuvenating, and creative powers. It will guide you to a better understanding of your inner wisdom and might even heal you, guide you to a healer, or teach you how to heal. Perhaps you will want to name them, or they will share their unique names with you. In any case, aligning with them signifies the beginning of a truly magical tree journey.

Aligning Your Staff with the Bird and Serpent Guardians of Your Tree of Life

Like the World Tree of Life, magic staffs have been depicted accompanied by the two tree guardians: the bird and the serpent. The serpent was sometimes concealed in the symbolism of ribbons and the bird in wings or as some other winged being.

While the magic staff represents the carrier's Tree of Life and its connection to the World Tree of Life, it is mainly a magical medium for channeling the otherworldly realms, beings, and our divine powers. The tree animals help animate the still energy of the staff and fortify its connection with the earthly and celestial realms. Once you meet the serpent and bird guardians of your Tree of Life, it's time to align them with your magic staff.

The serpent coiling around a staff is symbolic of the living energy field of the wood's original tree, but also the spiraling flow of the toroidal electromagnetic field of the World Tree of Life. That's why there are legends of staffs turning into serpents and vice versa. The serpent charges the staff with a vibrant earthly energy and helps it remain potent. Those who learn to differentiate between serpent guardians and the enemies of the tree (see Attuning to the Bird and Serpent Guardians of Your Tree of Life) can actually shield themselves from malevolent serpents using their tree staffs, as these block demonic entities.

After you become consciously aware of the bird and serpent guardians of your Tree of Life, simply invite them to work with you and your magic staff. It's best to do this during a contemplative walk with your staff as then you activate both the earthly energies (by pounding the staff on the ground) and the aerial one (by swaying the staff in the air). You will probably feel guided to do this after you have activated the four elements in your staff (see previous chapter) because the bird and serpent guardians are in tune with the earthly elements and elementals. Pounding the staff on the ground attracts the serpent guardians, other earthly animal guides, and earth deities, and simultaneously repels the demonic earthly forces. Elevating the staff in the air attracts the bird guardians, other aerial animal guides, and sky deities, and repels the demonic forces in outer space.

PART III

MAGIC OF INDIVIDUAL TREES

This part of the book is meant as a guide to the magical trees and the help and wisdom they offer to those who open their hearts to them.

11

Druidic Goddess Trees

Birch

Birch is one of the pioneer trees that recolonized Europe after the Ice Age and is usually one of the first tree species to forest areas that have been inhospitable thus far. It cleanses and nourishes the soil, providing wonderful conditions for other trees and plants to thrive in. It is because of this revitalizing quality that it has been regarded as a mother tree, a lady of the woods that fills its environment with life, light, and plenitude. Perhaps for that reason, goddesses such as Frigga, Freya, and Eostre have been associated with the birch. The ethereal light that its trunk and branches effuse is as spectacular in the moonlight as in sunlight, and it has inspired many artists and mystics.

Since birch loves water and its seeds are airborne, it's mainly associated with the air and water elements and ascribed with the properties of emotional and mental stimulation. For this reason, and the fact that its bark resembles paper, it's considered a symbolic tree for writers. However, most ancients believed that peeling off its bark could upset the spirit, and so the bark was harvested only once the tree had been "marked" by lightning as that was a benevolent sign of god Thor in Norse tradition or Perun in Slavic tradition.

Birch branches, bark, or leaves have also been incorporated into talismans that help us with emotional healing and psychic protection. Planting a birch near our home shields us from harm and malicious forces. In Celtic tradition, a protective cross of birch wood was made during Beltane, secured by a red ribbon, and hung from the highest spot at home. A broom made of young birch branches was used in ceremonial spirit cleansing to purify the energy field of an individual, home, or settlement.

This cleansing quality also applies to the healing properties of birch leaves, which have been used in natural medicine to flush out impurities, particularly bladder infections or kidney stones. Birch leaf infusions have also been recommended to induce sweating and lower fever.

Rowan

Rowan groves can be found in the vicinity of Celtic oracular shrines and stone circles, but it is not the tree's nature to create groups because it actually prefers other species as companions. In Anglo Saxon, rowan was called *cvicbeam* which means "life tree," and was therefore regarded as the Tree of Life. Its wood was used for spinning wheels and spindles, the attributes of the ancient fate goddesses. The tree is also linked with goddess Brigid who rules over spinning, and the spinning wheel was therefore one of her attributes.

Rowan likes to grow in higher altitudes and thrives even in quite inhospitable and inaccessible places on top of rocks or on the sides of mountains. For this reason, it has sometimes been called mountain ash. What the tree needs, however, is a lot of sunshine and fresh air, and that's why it has been linked with the elements of fire and air.

The berries have tiny pentagrams around their dimples, and this asymmetrical star has been regarded as a symbol of psychic protection. Perhaps it was because the rowan was marked by the magical pentagrams that it was believed to ward off evil. The Irish legend of Diarmuid and Grainne describes the rowan as the druidic tree that had grown from a berry of the elves, who were also called the "ever-living ones." Other legends mention dragon guardians living by rowan trees, but rowan itself makes a wonderful tree guardian.

Rowan staffs and wands were used for casting magic circles before rituals. Branches of rowan are believed to conceal sacred knowledge, and having one as a staff or a wand transmits profound wisdom to us. According to ancient tradition, it's best to ask the rowan spirit for such a magic tool during the summer solstice. A cross made of rowan and tied with a red ribbon in the center was believed to chase away evil.

The fruit was burned as incense for divination purposes and to chase away negative entities, curses, and sorcery. Rowan berry infusions have been used for visions, before astral travel, or for prophetic dreams. With the infusion comes an important warning, though: Like elderberries, rowan berries should only be consumed once cooked and can actually be toxic to us when eaten raw or in large quantities.

Rowan infusion was considered magical and was meant to be consumed modestly before meditations, journeys, and other rituals. It was also used as an antiseptic remedy, especially for sore throats or tonsillitis. The lady of the mountain, as the tree has sometimes been called, is a tree of freedom and overview that helps us find and pursue our spiritual mission here on earth. Being a hardy tree that prefers solitude, it is loved by hedge witches and hermits who, too, like to distance themselves from the hustle and bustle of society and focus their energy on their inner growth.

Willow

Willow needs a lot of water to thrive and therefore likes to grow by streams, ponds, or marshes. Myths and legends associate willows with the magic of the water element as well as the moon, and there is something truly magical about willows, especially at night. Czech folklore has a creature called Vodník, a water man with green skin and hands and the feet of a frog. Vodník likes to sit on a willow tree above ponds, but he can only be seen in the moonlight.

Traditionally, however, willow has been linked with goddesses, particularly the triple moon goddesses. Wise women, seers, and healers sought its company especially at night when the connection between water and the moon was strongest. It was then that a sacred threshold to the other realms was unveiled and the key to them – intuition – was activated.

Water is the element that offers the best reflection, and so along with the water medium, willow initiates us into the mystery of how this reality reflects the true home of our spirit. However, willow also inspires us to look beneath the surface. It's a tree of clairvoyance and prophecy. Touching willow and then placing the palm on the third eye is supposed to activate inner sight, and having a willow branch or piece of wood under a pillow at night helps us to receive its guidance in dreams.

Willow was also regarded as a wish-fulfilling tree and the tree to go to when performing rain-making rituals. Magic brooms were bound by willow branches, and weaving willow baskets was considered a meditative activity that enhanced psychic abilities. Willow was also believed to ward off bad luck and evil and was therefore planted near homes for this purpose. The tradition of knocking on wood actually comes from the Celtic tradition of knocking on a willow tree.

In natural medicine, willow was believed to treat health conditions derived from the damp such as arthritis or rheumatism. Moreover, willow helps us to heal deep, emotional issues, and crying under a willow was considered a cleansing ritual. Perhaps that's where the name weeping willow comes from.

During Samhain, willow helps us to connect with our ancestors and deceased loved ones or undergo a shamanic inner journey with them. Irish mythology regards harps made of willow wood as sacred instruments, and that's why they were used by the bards. The mission of bards was to transmit ancient myths and legends to people in artform, as well as to provide a connection with ancestors, nature spirits, and elves. Harp music was believed to help us tune in to ethereal realms and beings.

Apple

Apple comes from the rose family. The wild apple is called crab apple, and its fruit is relatively small (around two inches or five centimeters). In ancient times, apple trees had thorns and some still have them in the wild. Like hazel, apples have been considered the food of deities and a wonderful source of inspiration, creativity, and clarity.

Eating a wild apple or sitting under the tree's crown connects us to our divine selves and helps us attune to our inborn psychic gifts. This is reflected in the symbolic shape of its seeds and the ovary, as they both resemble the mandorla and the vesica piscis, an ancient symbol of the interdimensional gateway or the third eye.

However, the apple tree hides another mysterious symbol. It's not as apparent as in rowan berries, as it's only revealed to us when we cut its fruit in half widthways. Then, we find that its core and seeds are arranged into the pentagram, the symbol of life force, creation, divine wisdom, and protection.

The fruit, however, is magical both on a spiritual and on a physical level as apples are a good source of iron, potassium, and vitamin A and E, with most of the vitamins and minerals being found right under the skin. Apples help us cleanse the organs, especially the digestive system and kidneys, but they also help with nausea, headaches, and high blood pressure. The healing benefit of apples is summed up in the proverb "An apple a day keeps the doctor at bay." In mythology, we read of various magical apples that were sacred to the deities and were believed to promote longevity, even immortality. The Celtic Isle of Avalon, also called Avallon or Afallon, actually translates as "the isle of apple trees." It was a mystical island of endless spring where great healers lived under the rulership of Queen Argante.

Apple was adored by the Sidhe, elves, and many deities such as the Welsh goddess Arwen, British Gwen, Greek Aphrodite, Hera, and Nemesis – who had an apple staff – and the Jewish Shekinah who presided over sacred apples. In the ancient patriarchal legends, apple trees had serpent guardians that were killed before the tree was ravished. In ancient Greek mythology, Hercules killed the serpent guardian of the sacred apple tree in the Garden of the Hesperides and stole the magical apples; in ancient Mesopotamia, Gilgamesh felled an apple tree that was a home to Lilith, the sacred serpent, and a bird; and in the Bible, a serpent offering Eve the apple of temptation became a symbol for sin.

Apples are connected to the following pagan festivals: Beltane, during which the trees are planted; Litha, as that is the time when mistletoe is found in its branches; Mabon, the beginning of the apple harvest; and Samhain, when the harvest is completed. The last apple is traditionally left on the tree as a gift to the apple tree spirit. And it's truly magical to see an apple tree with a single apple hanging from its bare branches, as it feels like the promise of a new beginning.

ELDER

Although now elders rarely grow higher than seventy-eight inches (two meters), in ancient times, their crown reached up to three hundred and fifty inches (nine meters) above the ground. They are very hardy and can actually regrow and regenerate from the healthy parts of their roots and thrive even in poor soil and shade.

Many ancients believed that elder was protected by a group spirit which they called Elder Mother, Lady Elder, or simply Elle. Folk traditions say that this spirit should be asked three times before you take a part of her trees and, even then, you should be wary of taking too much because she hates greed and selfishness. The spirit is very protective of her physical forms and seeks revenge on those who cut her wood or burn it without her approval. That's why gypsies never burned elder. Elder sees right into our hearts, and if we respect her, she shares her wisdom and healing power with us.

The ancient Greeks, Romans, and even Celts believed that elder could cure all human diseases. In Russia, elder was used extensively during plagues as it was believed to chase away illness and evil. In some parts of Switzerland and Southern Germany, villagers still touch their hats when they pass elders or say "Hats off to the elder!" to pay their respects to her spirit. The Native Americans considered elder to be the mother of humanity, and in Norse mythology, the first woman, Embla, was made from an elder tree (though some suggest it might have been elm or vine). Her feminine energy is supported by the fact that she's been affiliated to goddess Venus (Greek Aphrodite).

The Celts believed that fairies appeared to those who fell asleep under an elder tree during Midsummer Night, and that if special talismans against bewitchment such as a piece of iron weren't at hand, you could be wooed into the fairy lands. The fragrance of elder blossom was believed to transport the spirit into the netherworld and was therefore considered a wonderful guide during deep meditation or journeying. According to Celtic folklore, elder nymphs tend to appear to those who approach them with a loving intention, especially during the full moon. It is also said that lightning supposedly never hits elder, and so its berries were hung up in homes to protect the dwellings from lightning strikes.

The graceful and healing quality of elder was tainted during the medieval Catholic Christianization period in Europe. Like many magical trees, elder became a feared witch tree and her spirit started to be portrayed as an evil hag. The fact that her spirit guarded her physical forms with such verve made people think she hated humankind altogether. Scary tales were told back then that were probably meant to deter people from elder. For example, it was said that elder was the tree on which Judas hung himself or that its wood was used for crucifixion crosses.

If the berries survive on the elder until December, they are supposedly even more potent and ready for a special, fortune-telling infusion. Elder was also believed to chase away evil entities including those of the interdimensional or extraterrestrial kind.

No part of elder should be consumed fresh as it contains cyanide, which is destroyed by boiling. Elderberry tea is a known herbal remedy against coughs and colds because it reduces fever and promotes sweating. Moreover, elder blossom has been used in creams because of its strong anti-wrinkle properties. Elderberries cooked in flaxseed oil supposedly help treat hemorrhoids.

Elder is also a wonderful healer on an emotional level. Meditating next to elder appeases fearful thoughts and protects us from negativity. That's why elders were planted near homes where they became powerful shields and even attracted wealth to the household if treated with respect. Furthermore, elder was believed to protect pregnant women and newborn children, and in ancient times, women kissed the tree to ensure a good birth and bless the child with vibrant health. The ogham name means "red" or "to redden" (possibly blush).

Beech

The Celts considered beech the mother of the forest, a counterpart to oak who was its father. Beech has a truly nurturing quality as it fertilizes the soil and provides welcoming conditions for other plants. To fully demonstrate that she's the lady of the woodlands, beech wears her wide, rich crown proudly on top of her distinctly smooth trunk.

Beech also produces very nutritious nuts, though it takes about fifty years for the tree to be ready to harvest. Our ancestors used to consume these nuts, hence the ancient Greek name for beech *phegos*, which actually relates to *phagein*, the word that translates as "eating." Roasted beech nuts and the protein-rich beech leaves can be used as a garnish, but you should be very careful not to eat too many of them in a fresh form as they contain a toxic saponin called glycoside, which is only destroyed by cooking. The nuts, which ripen during late summer and early autumn, have also been used for making cooking oil and as a substitute for coffee, without the energizing effect.

In ancient times, very thin tablets of beech were used as an alternative to scrolls. In German, beech is *buche* and book *buch*, and the Anglo-Saxon word for beech – *bok* – is the same as "book," so there's a clear language connection as well. Moreover, *buchstaben* meaning "beech sticks" is a German word for letters, and in Old Slavic the word *bukvice* was used both for "letters" and "beech nuts." For this reason, beech has been regarded as the tree of writers and poets. Besides the name's literal connection to writing, beeches are believed to hold local tales and wisdom.

Beech is known as a wish-fulfilling tree. If the tree spirit likes you and empathizes with your desires, she may help you. Whispering a wish to a beech or writing it on a piece of paper and burying it in the soil nearby is an ancient magical practice.

In natural medicine, beech has been used for skin diseases and eczema. Since beech leaves have a cooling effect, they have also been known to reduce swelling and lower fever, and placing them under sheets to soothe the patient was a common practice in the olden days.

12

Druidic God Trees

Oak

Oak is a hardy tree that is able to outlive most other species except for yew. The fact that it grows and matures slowly is what makes its wood so strong and resilient. Ivy likes to coil around oak trunks for support, complementing the bark that is often covered in beautiful shades of lichen. All these factors make oak look grand even after death.

The oak crown grows very wide and so do its roots, which makes this tree the perfect prototype for the Celtic Tree of Life where the crown reflects the roots. The Celts considered oak to be the king of the forest or the father tree. The ancient Greeks believed oak to be the first created tree. One of the oldest oracles, Dodona, was built around a massive oak dedicated to the father god Zeus, mother goddess Dione, and the prophetesses called Peleiades, who were sometimes referred to as "the doves" after the sacred bird.

According to archeologists, the oracle was a place of prophecy that was probably intuited from oracular sounds such as the rustling of the oak leaves or the chiming of sacred bronze objects hung from the branches. Oak was linked to other thunder gods besides Zeus, such as Perun, Thor, or Taranis. The thunder gods had powerful weapons that used the electric charge of lightning to strike their enemy. The truth is that oak has a strong electrical current and lightning tends to strike it more often than other trees.

In ancient times, oak forests spread all over Europe and were venerated by Baltic, Slavic, Germanic, and Celtic tribes who liked to gather in oak groves. The Druids revered oaks and often marked the most magical oaks with an encircled cross – one of the oldest World Tree of Life symbols. Oak mistletoe is still traditionally gathered during the winter solstice. It was called *druad-lus* which means "Druid's plant." However, the association between Druids and oaks seems to come from only one source – a Roman military commander, Pliny the Elder. The old Irish and Gaelic word for oak is *duir* or *dair*, which could be a riddle for "Druid," but could also relate to *duir*, a Sanskrit word for door. Like most trees, oak was believed to conceal an entrance into the otherworldly realms and was considered the king of such thresholds.

The Romans believed that humans were born from tree trunks, especially oak. They had a sacred oak tree growing on Capitoline Hill dedicated to god Jupiter (equivalent to Greek Zeus). Oak spirits were believed to resemble cheerful looking, wrinkly old men who spread humor and mischief and took revenge on those who mistreated the woodlands. This idea has been encapsulated in the Green Man.

Oak has a fatherly energy, and sitting by it or hugging it gives us a sense of comfort and security. Oaks were also a source of nutrition for our ancestors as acorns were used for making flour and a bitter, coffee-like drink. As for natural healing, oak leaves were known to treat wounds and inflammation. Moreover, a decoction of acorns or oak bark was believed to be an antidote to plant poisoning. Like ash, oak was mainly linked to the fire element, light, and the sun.

Holly

Holly is a beautiful evergreen that may reach up to five hundred and ninety inches (fifteen meters) in height especially if it grows as a solitaire. In woodlands, it's often seen among oak and beech trees. Holly is mainly known for its bright red berries that are, however, toxic to humans and most animals except for birds.

It was considered unlucky to fell holly or harm it in any way, but a small branch was traditionally brought inside during the winter solstice as its red berries helped to light up the dark days. There's a pagan tradition linked to holly that survived early medieval Christianization, which is that the holly's spirit is the holly king of the woods. The holly king and oak king were the symbolic expression of the light and dark halves of the year. The holly king, previously known simply as the psychopomp, or the god of the netherworld, ruled in the dark half of the year (from the summer solstice to the winter solstice) and the oak king, the god of the earth and sky, ruled in the light part (from the winter solstice to the summer solstice).

Both the kings are an expression of the Green Man, an archetype of the woodland spirit later called Jack in the Green or the May king as he was the one who carried the maypole. The maypole tradition replaced an even more ancient one during which it was not just a pole but a living tree that was ceremonially brought and planted in the center of a settlement and whose spirit became the local guardian. Green Man folklore was one of the few pagan traditions that was adapted by medieval Catholic Christianity. It was depicted covered in foliage, mainly that of oak and holly, and its face decorated the facades and interiors of churches.

During the darkest times of the year, holly branches were taken home to attract cheerful fairy folk inside abodes, but they were given back to the woodlands before Imbolc. Holly branches were also used in the Roman tradition of Saturnalia, during which a celebration of Saturn returning to its native Capricorn star sign was celebrated.

Planting a holly tree near to homes shielded against envious people, evil spirits, and even lightning bolts. Meditating with holly helps us delve into our subconscious and bring to light important insights. The spirit of holly may even guide us to look into deeper, emotional issues if we are ready to face them. Along with the birch, holly is a tree of new beginnings, hope, and renewal. Curiously, the holly ogham actually means "iron pole."

Hazel

Hazel grows in damp places, especially near streams or ponds, but it can also be found above secluded underground water and springs. Its branches have been used for dowsing, especially with the help of pixies. Pilgrims often carried hazel staffs and were even buried with them.

Hazel is an important tree in Celtic, Greek, and Roman mythologies. To the Celts, hazel was a tree of knowledge and wisdom, and perhaps that's why one of the three earliest rulers of Ireland and the last king of the Tuatha de Danann was called Mac Cuill, which means "son of hazel."

There's an old Irish story about Connla's Well that has two versions. One tells us of nine magical hazels that grow around a sacred well and when the nuts drop into the water, they are eaten by magical salmon that begin to glow upon swallowing them. In the other version, the well is located under the sea at the source of the River Shannon. There, the father of all salmon found nine magical hazelnuts, and after he ate them, he received wisdom and sacred knowledge from the guardians of the well. This well of wisdom may parallel with the well of ancestral memory where the Norse god Odin received his initiation in runes. Nevertheless, salmon represent swiftness and a connection between the water and air elements as these fish swim very fast and often leap into the air.

Hazelnuts were considered the food of deities. Some ancient gods had an even more profound connection to hazel, though. The name of the Roman forest god Silvanus comes from the Latin word *sylvestris* which means "hazel." The messenger gods Hermes and Mercury carried a hazel staff that was given to them by the sun god Apollo. The staff, called the caduceus, had wings atop and was entwined by two serpents, though these were sometimes replaced by ribbons. Hazel helps us attune to these gods, who share some common traits such as mischievousness and a love of nature. Both Hermes and Mercury are also powerful psychopomps and therefore, along with hazel, they make wonderful guides during inner journeys.

The group spirit of hazel teaches us about the magic of communication, art, and alchemy. It's the patron of artists and those who work with their imagination. The Celts regarded hazel as a tree of bards and ovades. Druids celebrated hazel trees mainly during Mabon, the ninth month of harvest that marked the end of summer. Magic staffs made of hazel represented personal creative powers, and fork-shaped hazel wands were used for fortune telling.

Meditating and journeying with hazel can have a profound effect, especially on an emotional and mental level. Some mystics believe that the group spirit of hazel, along with its guardian gods, Hermes and Mercury, answer even the most peculiar questions in the form of insights and synchronicity. However, make sure you are ready for a powerful download of information because such messages tend to be generous and fast. Overall, hazel helps us speed things up, especially when it comes to creativity.

Hazelnuts are full of omega-3 and omega-6 fatty acids, vitamin E, and protein. This makes them a very nutritious snack. In natural medicine, hazelnuts are used to cure coughs, sore throats, and fever, especially when mixed with honey.

Alder

Alder loves water and thrives mainly next to rivers, streams, and ponds. It may actually grow partly in a body of water, which makes the wood almost stone-like in appearance, and its roots then create perfect shelters for fish and frogs. Since alder makes the best charcoal, it has also been linked with the fire element, but its power lies in the vivifying energy of the water element.

Alder is the only broadleaf tree species with cones that, like pinecones, visually remind us of the pineal gland and therefore symbolically link to the third eye and inner seeing. The alder guides us to a better intuition and to psychic powers, and it helps us deal with deep emotional issues and subconscious processes.

The Celtic and Germanic cultures saw alder as the elf king of the woods whose spirit could shape-shift into a raven or crow when disturbed. Interestingly, the wood has a red sap and looks like it's bleeding when cut. Our ancient ancestors never felled alders because they were aware of their shape-shifting abilities and didn't want to upset the natural spirits. Alder was also the tree of the Irish hero Bran who, too, was associated with ravens.

Alder's hardiness and special connection to the water element makes the alder cones, branches, and leaves wonderful luck charms for strengthening psychic abilities. Meditating with alder deepens our prophetic powers and our connection with nature spirits, and might even make the elves notice us. Alder's spirit inspires a deep empathy and respect for nature and all its beings. It's common to feel gratitude in its presence or experience a sudden realization of how certain beings or places could use your care and protection.

In natural medicine, alder leaf infusions were used to treat inflammation and swelling, and especially to soothe painful tonsils or gums. An alder cone is a perfect talisman for meditations and for starting inner dialogues with elves. It even helps us attain a better inner seeing and hearing.

Pine

Conifers are ancient trees that were on this planet long before the broadleaved trees. Though originally many conifers were native to the UK and continental Europe in the last interglacial period, during the time of the Celts there was only pine in the woodlands (Scot's pine with a reddish bark and deep fissures). Fir and spruce were brought between the 16th and 17th centuries from Scandinavia.

Vikings were buried in dragon ships made of pine wood and the Celts revered pine as well. Legend has it that the wizard Merlin climbed the Pine of Barenton, which gave him profound knowledge, and he has not returned to earth since. Merlin's tree enlightenment correlates to that of god Odin or Buddha.

Pine has been held sacred in many cultures, and pinecones were often depicted in association with various Mesopotamian, Egyptian, Indian, and Greek deities. The Assyrian Tree of Life was guarded by winged gods holding pinecones, and both Buddha and Shiva have been portrayed with pinecones on their heads. Moreover, pinecones are often seen on the tops of sacred staffs or wands, mainly those of the nature gods such as Osiris, Pan, Bacchus, or Dionysus. In magic, pinecones symbolize the third eye or the pineal gland, which was named after the pine for its uncanny resemblance to it.

Pines have a strong presence in the wintertime as they don't shed their leaves and they keep the landscape green all year long. The evergreen nature of conifers reminds us of the eternal, renewing qualities of nature that are present in everything within and around us. Taoist monks consider pine nuts a holy food whose nutrition supposedly conceals the secret to eternal life.

In natural medicine, pine seeds and buds were picked in the springtime and were believed to cure coughs and bronchitis. Both the Native American Hopi and the Celts believed that pine needles protected us against evil. Therefore, pine branches have been kept at home, mainly above entrances, for protection from curses or sorcery and once dry, the pine needles have been used for smudging homes in order to chase off bad moods and troubling thoughts.

13

Other Druidic Trees, Bushes, and Lianas

Yew

We could say that yew is one of the most unique trees as it can be considered neither a broadleaf nor a conifer because "conifer" translates as "cone-bearing tree" and yew doesn't bear any cones. Instead, yew produces red fruit that is, like all parts of the tree, deadly poisonous. Perhaps for that reason, yew has been known as the tree of death even though on a deeper level, it is actually associated with immortality.

Yews were one of the first evergreens to grow in the primeval forests. They mature very slowly but are incredibly hardy if they are left to thrive. Some yews are believed to be a few thousand years old, but it's hard to guess how old some yews are exactly, as they continuously renew themselves. Yews have an incredible self-sustaining, self-rejuvenating quality, which lies in the power of their roots that grow through the old, decaying trunk and support a new trunk that rises from the hollow bark of the original tree.

And to amaze us even more, yew branches tend to grow down into the ground, form new roots, and thus complete the image of the Celtic Tree of Life where the roots and branches are entwined. This evokes the self-sufficient quality of the torus and the natural electromagnetic fields. Perhaps that's why yew is more fit to be the World Tree in Norse mythology because it was described as an evergreen ash, but most scholars consider this expression just an old name for the yew tree.

The roots are the pivotal base of all trees, but yews demonstrate their power with all their might. For this reason, yews may connect us to our own roots and ancestral wisdom as well as providing inner guidance from previous incarnations.

Yew trees are also the guardians of the thresholds between the earthly and ethereal worlds, even the afterlife. Since they were believed to connect us with the otherworldly realms and with our departed loved ones, they were planted in graveyards and sought between Samhain (today known as Halloween) and Yule (the winter solstice). This darkest time of the year is the best time for spiritism and channeling our ancestral spirit guides. It was considered very unlucky to fell a yew tree, like all magic trees, especially since they were the trees of eternal life.

Yews inspire us to work with our natural self-sustaining and self-revitalizing energy field which is generated by the Odic force and the electromagnetic field of the heart (see chapters two and seven). Moreover, the yew may guide us to a symbolic rebirth on a spiritual level as meditating with it helps us awaken to new levels of awareness.

ASH

The ash crown grows very tall and wide and reflects its roots, which spread far and deep. Although some historical records point to the yew tree as the prototype of the "evergreen ash" as the World Tree in Norse mythology, ash is likewise a wonderful example of the Tree of Life. The ash tree was held sacred by the Norse tribes, and the Anglo Saxons even called the Vikings *Æscling* which means "the men of ash."

Ash wisdom has been linked with the ceaseless exchange between the past and the future since in a mystical sense, the future could be seen as a corrected, bettered past. Ash is a perfect companion for shamanic journeys and could perhaps even be a time-traveling mediator for more experienced magicians.

Since ash loves to grow in the vicinity of clear water sources and the Greek god Poseidon was believed to adore its wood, sailors have used it as a luck charm during their voyages. Like willow, ash twigs were also used in rain-making ceremonies.

Though ash can grow in any soil and tolerate even windy locations, it needs a lot of water and sun to thrive. In Czech, its name *jasan* means "the shining one" as *jas* means "shine." For that reason, ash has been affiliated with the sun and the fire element, which complements the opposite water energy association. Another connection to the fire element is the fact that ash trees are often struck by lightning. In Norse legend, the thunder god Thor was saved by an ash while almost drowning in the river that led into the netherworld (this could, by the way, be another river reference to the interdimensional channels discussed in chapter two).

Since in Norse mythology ash was the tree from which Odin

created the first man, it was considered to have a masculine energy. Ash is also the tree of the Welsh hero Gwydion, an illustrious Druid, alchemist, magician, and trickster who shares some traits with gods Odin, Hermes, and Mercury. In magic tradition, ash wands and staffs helped with healing and exorcism. However, there were also goddesses linked with ash trees. In Greek mythology, ash was the tree of the nymphs called the Meliae and the ash branch was one of the main attributes of Nemesis, the goddess of fate and justice and a sister of the Moirai who epitomize the triple goddess, Fates, or Norns.

Ash has edible, nutritious leaves, but as they are not easily digestible, a leaf infusion is preferable in natural medicine. Our ancestors drank ash tea for strength, flexibility, and longevity as well as for treating rheumatism and gout. In British tradition, clippings of a person's nail were buried under an ash to help that person heal, especially from fever or toothache. Moreover, meditating or sitting by an ash tree was believed to heal past trauma or refresh old thought patterns.

Since ash comes from the olive family, it ties in to the magical power of the olive tree mentioned in chapter fourteen.

Elm

Some say that the ogham Ailim refers to conifers while others say it's associated with the elm. Either way, elms were mentioned in many Celtic legends and used to dominate the landscape of ancient Europe and America.

Elms have a fascinating, widespread root system. The young trees evolve from the roots of their parent trees and remain connected to the wide root system of their kin even after they mature. Elm roots are known to fertilize – even heal – the soil that they grow from, and that's why all vegetation thrives in their vicinity. In magic, elms represent healing, rejuvenation, and rebirth but also the connection to our family, kin, ancestors, and our past lives.

Elms were also associated with the netherworld. However, once this ethereal realm of nature spirits was later demonized and called hell, many people avoided elms. Celts saw elms as gateways into the realms of the elves, hidden people, or the Sidhe who were also believed to live beneath rocks and mountains. Elms were planted on ancient burial mounds or on graves in the hope of attracting the spiritual guidance of the fairy folk who would look after the souls of the departed. In Old English, elms were called *elven* or *elfin* and the tree's German folk name is *elfenholz* which means "elven wood."

In the 10th century, during the crucial Catholic Christianization of Britain, a canon of the Saxon king Edgar declared that the worship of elms, as well as communicating and divination with the spirits through elms, should be banned. Since then, this tree species was referred to as the "witch elm," which only proves the tree's profound meaning to the ancients. After a few more fearful superstitions were created, elms became even more affiliated with death rather than life, and to consolidate this, coffins were made from elm wood. The healing, rejuvenating power of the elm was seemingly lost, and even its ogham symbol, the cross, became a symbol of death instead of the Tree of Life that it originally represented.

And finally, long after that, the large grid of elm woods and hedgerows was destroyed by Dutch elm disease that spread in 1919. Luckily, elms have begun to thrive in Europe and hopefully will create their magical grid of protection and healing energy field once again.

Elm seeds are rich in minerals and proteins and can be eaten fresh or cooked. Their shape resembles the sacred symbol of vesica piscis or mandorla, which like the elm tree represents the gateway into the otherworldly realms. In Norse mythology, the first woman, Embla, was believed to have been created either from elder or elm, though some theories even link the name to the vine and liana.

Aspen

Aspen comes from the poplar family of fast-growing but not very long-lived trees. The "quaking aspen" may be mistaken for the birch tree, but its bark does not peel off as easily as that of a birch. It also prefers solitude and doesn't like to be shaded by other trees. It stands out in meadows or moors away from human settlements The tree is believed to enjoy the company of animals, and for that reason it was the perfect tree to meditate or journey with when connecting with one's spirit animals.

We may easily tune in to the realm of magical animals and nature spirits when gazing at the ethereal halo that surrounds an aspen's crown and the soft shimmer of its leaves, which tremble even in the slightest movement of wind. The gentle rustling sound of its branches sounds like the whisper of fairies, and perhaps that's the reason why aspen has mainly been associated with the air element, air elementals, air nymphs, and the messenger god Hermes (Roman Mercury). Artists may find a lot of inspiration near aspen as it's considered a powerful vision tree.

To the ancients, aspen was also important for its profound

shielding power. Aspens were planted near homes or settlements to repel evil and harm. The Native American Hopi used dry aspen leaves for smudging and the Celts even used aspen wood for war shields. Aspen has also been known as a tree of comfort that soothes the spirit and chases away fear and anxiety.

Like elm, aspen has, too, been known to conceal secret entrances into the fairy realms and the netherworld. The Catholic Church tried to hide the aspen's magical power by making it a tree of fear and death rather than life. According to medieval superstitions, aspen leaves trembled because its wood was used for crucifixion crosses.

Aspen leaves contain salicylic acid and are therefore used as anti-inflammatory and antibacterial medicine. Herbal medicine recommends chewing its leaves to relieve pain and fever. The aspen ogham, Eadha, links both to aspen and white poplar.

White Poplar

White poplar has a truly ethereal appearance with its smooth, light gray trunk, and bright green leaves that are silvery-white on the underside and create a beautiful spectacle when they tremble in the wind. Our ancient ancestors considered the leaves magical because they grow in the shape of a five-pointed star, a symbol of creation, wisdom, and protection. Maybe for that reason a white poplar leaf infusion was consumed before astral travel. Poplar leaves were, however, also used for money spells as they were believed to attract abundance. During late October, the period of Samhain, dried poplar leaves were used in smudging to clear up old energies and welcome the new sun that was to rise during the winter solstice.

In mythology, both white poplar and aspen have been linked with Persephone, a goddess of the earth as well as the netherworld who balances the light and dark sides of the world. Persephone legendarily had a poplar grove at her home in the land of sunset.

HAWTHORN

Hawthorn is a small tree or shrub of the rose family that seems to like human company as it prefers to grow in hedgerows and villages rather than in woodlands. Hawthorn has a welcoming, nurturing energy that attracts many birds and insects. In fact, its crown may host more than thirty species of insects.

Hawthorn has been regarded as the shrub of love, fertility, and marriage. Celts used to perform wedding rituals under blooming hawthorns around the Beltane festival. They also used the bright red berries that ripen in the early autumn as decoration and hung hawthorn garlands above the newly-weds' bed to ensure lasting affection between them.

Hawthorn likes to grow by springs and wells but is not picky when it comes to soil and can adapt to even dry and windy places. The leaves are edible and actually taste very good in salads. In natural healing, the hawthorn berry infusion was believed to cleanse the bloodstream and treat all kinds of heart and kidney conditions. The florets were used to soothe sore throats and inflamed tonsils.

The tree is linked with Cardea, an Italian goddess who presides over pregnant women and infants. She blessed children and harmonized their male and female energies. Cardea's consort was Janus, who likewise governed marriage, childbirth, the seasonal cycles, and the harvest. Moreover, hawthorn pertains to the Welsh goddess Olwen who was sometimes referred to as the White Goddess who left behind tracks of hawthorn florets as she walked the universe; her magic footprints legendarily became the spiral of the Milky Way. The holy Glastonbury thorn that legendarily grew from the magic staff of Joseph of Arimathea is also of the hawthorn species.

Blackthorn

Blackthorn is a shrub that often grows in hedgerows with hawthorn, and for that reason the two species are often confused. Blackthorn branches are much thornier, though, and the bark is very dark, almost black. Blackthorn represents life's polarity, the yin and yang, action and reaction, dark and light, and so forth. Its thorny branches make a great shelter for birds as it protects them from predators. In magic, blackthorn also has a highly protective power and is therefore a profound helper in shielding rituals. Its fruit and branches make wonderful talismans against negativity, sorcery, and evil.

The shrub has been mainly linked with the planets Mars and Saturn. Mars is the reckless rebel who inspires our inner spirit warrior while Saturn teaches us about destiny, justice, and order. When these two energies are misunderstood, they can cause a lot of tension, but when in harmony, they result in balanced allies. In an individual, this reflects in the ability to live by free will. A person should do this wisely so as not to be a victim or a master of others; ultimately, you should only be a master of yourself.

Blackthorn blossoms very early and, depending on the weather conditions, sometimes shows off its first blooms in February. The blackthorn sloes are astringent but rich in vitamin C and are a natural cure for inflammation, particularly tonsillitis. They are best picked after the first frost, but because of their intensely sour taste, they are added to jams or syrups. In natural medicine, the leaves and flowers are used to treat stomach problems or indigestion as they are believed to clear our digestive tract of toxins.

Blackthorn blossom, as well as hawthorn, was used in fertility rites during the Beltane festival, but its energy rather suits the time of Samhain, the darkest time of the year when both our shadow side and inner light are most active and need to be balanced.

Gorse/Furze

Gorse, also called furze, is a shrub that grows abundantly on moors, heaths, rocks, and hillsides. It tolerates poor soil and drought but needs plenty of sunlight to thrive. Owing to its nitrogen-fixing ability, gorse may even rejuvenate soil in barren, rocky areas where no other plants previously grew and become a supporter of other plant life in its vicinity.

Gorse is highly flammable, but it is a pyrophyte and therefore fire tolerant. Its burnt stumps sprout again after wildfires and its seed pods pop open in the intense heat and spread new seeds. This fire resistance is what has always fascinated people about gorse. It was sacred to the Druids who admired its ability to withstand destruction by fire and go on creating new life no matter what. To the alchemists, gorse represented the transmutation of common metals into gold, which symbolized the process of enlightenment on a spiritual level.

Another amazing fact about gorse is that its pollen-rich blossom keeps blooming from springtime throughout the summer and makes a wonderful home for bees who adore its sweet nectar. Moreover, gorse hosts many bird species, and these like to build nests in its thorny branches where they can find seclusion from predators. The blossom gives out a special vanilla, almost coconut-like, scent.

Gorse's bright yellow florets have been worn as talismans and were believed to attract abundance both on a physical and spiritual level. Gorse is, however, mainly the shrub of optimism and joy that brings about good moods and feelings of deep gratitude. It inspires positive thinking and boosts our power center, the solar chakra.

In the olden days, gorse ash mixed with clay was used as soap. Because of its golden color, favorable taste, and scent, the blossom has been used in cooking, but it's important to note that all parts of the plant should be eaten in moderation as they contain toxic alkaloids that may cause high blood pressure and other heart issues.

Gorse seeds soaked in water supposedly make a great fly repellent. Curiously, its ogham name, Onn, originally links to the ash tree, and in the modern ogham alphabet it has even been linked with heather, but gorse is an important druidic shrub nonetheless.

Ivy

Ivy is a climbing shrub that coils around other trees for support. It could be compared to a soul wandering through the World Tree of Life, seeking to be unified with the all. Ivy adapts to a variety of conditions, all kinds of soil, and even shade. It has an inborn determination and can be hardy and persistent if it's allowed to grow. Ivy represents curiosity and adaptability, but also the importance of companionship and support in this harsh world. However, since ivy can weaken and even destroy its host tree if it feeds on its nutrients and sunlight, it teaches us not to be selfish and to live in harmony with our surroundings.

Along with the other evergreens, ivy symbolizes the eternity of life and spirit, and that's why Druids placed its branches on their altars. The winding growth pattern of ivy reminds us of the sacred spiral of life and serpentine powers. Its leaves form a five-pointed star, which complements the spiral in the symbolism of progress, manifestation, and psychic protection. In woodlands, it creates dense, mysterious enclosures and reminds us of fairytale labyrinths that take heroes on a path within in order to learn something about themselves.

Ivy branches were believed to attract benevolent devas and nature spirits. However, since ivy is very poisonous, it has not been used in natural medicine. Ivy's ogham name is Gort, which actually means "field," but the Proto-Indo-European root is *ghost* that translates as "enclosure" and links to the ivy's symbolic uniting quality.

Grapevine

Like ivy, grapevine is another climbing shrub that coils around other trees for support and usually ties together multiple plants as if aiming to bring them closer. In this regard, both ivy and grapevine represent the spiral and serpent symbolism as well as the DNA double helix, or kundalini energy.

Grapevine needs plenty of light to produce grapes, which ripen between the summer festival, Lammas, and the first autumn festival, Mabon. The grapes represent harvest and were consumed during wealth and abundance rituals.

In mythology, vine has been linked with deities such as Greek Dionysus or Roman Bacchus who both loved wilderness, plenitude, and virility. They were also associated with the sensually driven nature spirits called satyrs. It's curious that both Dionysus and Bacchus were depicted with a staff called a thyrsus that usually had serpents, ribbons, or a vine coiled around it and was crowned with a pinecone, which links to the pineal gland and the third eye. Both the gods, along with many other nature spirits, were believed to enjoy wine, and that's why the intoxicating beverage was brought to the groves as an offering to attract their attention.

Grapes are full of antioxidants, flavonoids, vitamins, and copper. Moreover, drinking wine, though in moderation, has been known to cleanse the blood. The original ogham word for vine, Muin, actually translates as "the upper part of the spine," which could relate to serpentine symbolism and kundalini energy, but it also means "love."

Broom

Broom is a hardy shrub that prefers dry soil and plenty of sunshine. Its leafless stems produce yellow flowers and eventually turn into seed capsules.

Broom has been used for making broomsticks, which are tools affiliated with witches in European folklore and fairy tales. It's possible that brooms were magic staffs in disguise because both brooms and staffs have been associated with interdimensional travel. However, tales of wizards with tree staffs and witches with broomsticks could hide a patriarchal motive to degrade the magical powers of women. After all, as Max Dashu pointed out in her book *Witches and Pagans*, magic staffs of many acclaimed female healers and psychics have been incorrectly interpreted as household tools in the past.

Along with smudging, broomsticks have been used to cleanse a space of negativity, and sweeping the floor can become a magical act of purification. You can easily make yourself a magic broomstick by binding stalks of broom tightly together and fastening them to a branch. The broomstick may then be decorated with charms and symbols that ensure an even stronger purging.

Broom was also traditionally used as a decoration at weddings with the intention of sweeping away jealousy and envy. In the ogham, the broom sign is NGetal, which in neopagan traditions actually represents reed. As opposed to the broom, reed grows in damp locations but is also symbolically linked with cleansing, particularly on an emotional level.

Heather

The ogham sign Úr means "earth" or "soil" as well as "moisture" and "damp ground," but it's been most commonly associated with heather. Heather is a low shrub that likes acidic soil, and though it grows mainly on moors, it also thrives in oak or pine forest glades. Because of its beautiful shades of pink and purple, it has an association with the crown chakra and is believed to have a calming, soothing effect.

In magic, heather is thought to attract love and provide inspiration as well as a better connection to the ethereal realms. In natural medicine, heather florets and leaves are used as an infusion to cleanse and support the kidneys and the urinary tract. The ogham Úr could parallel the Norse rune Uruz, the rune of strength, vitality, healing, and the water element.

14

Sacred Trees of Other Traditions

Linden

Linden is an old Anglo-Saxon name for this magical tree, also sometimes called "lime" due to the soft, lime-colored light that its leaves emit early in the summer. It's a hardy, vigorous tree that may live for a very long time in the right conditions. In many ways, it could be compared to the oak, and in fact, to the ancient Slavs, linden was the queen to the oak king.

Linden's intoxicatingly fragrant, cream-colored florets bloom in late June to July, during which it also hosts many types of bees. Linden nymphs like to move around and may often visit you if you've been granted a linden staff.

To the ancient Norse and Germanic tribes, linden was the tree of goddesses Freya and Frigga who might actually be the same deity. Freya, the goddess cloaked in feathers who loved to roam the wilderness with her two male cats, brought the Aesir gods the gift of *seiðr*, which is Norse shamanism and magic that involves both predicting and shaping future events. Like Freya, linden represents love, care, and motherly affection. This even shows in its leaves, which are heart shaped.

Furthermore, in natural medicine, linden leaves and blossom are used to treat heart conditions as it is believed to purify the bloodstream and lower blood pressure. It's also been used to reduce fever during the common cold and be effective in cleansing and soothing the sinuses. On a psychological level, it has a calming effect and can treat anxiety or hyperactivity. As Fred Hageneder points out in his book *The Living Wisdom of Trees*, the German word *lindern* actually means "to soothe."

Linden leaves were usually fed to cattle, but humans can consume them as well, for they are quite nutritious and tasty. They can be tossed in salads in the spring or summertime when the leaves are still soft and easy to chew.

The linden is a national tree of Czechia, and therefore it is patron and guardian of many Bohemian and Moravian villages. Some say linden is the tree of the legendary Libuše, an ancient queen and prophetess who founded Prague after having a vision of its future glory. A beautiful old linden also grows in the middle of Prague's Saint Agnes convent, symbolizing Agnes's powerful, caring spirit and her profound connection with nature.

Cherry

Cherry is regarded as the tree of love mainly for its beautiful, pink blossom and its fruit that grows in pairs. Interestingly, if we keep them that way, the fruit is more likely to stay fresh for longer. In Japan, the tree has been venerated as a tree of romance, fertility, and new beginnings. The blossom is used as a traditional wedding drink called *sakurayu* (cherry blossom tea). In Czech tradition, couples kiss under a cherry tree on May 1 to bless their union. In magic, cherries were known to help with love, as well as to balance the god and the goddess energies because the tree has both feminine and masculine qualities and is the epitome of the alchemical sacred marriage.

In natural medicine, cherries were used to treat gout and to relieve pain. The leaf infusion was believed to keep the body healthy and protected from infection. In traditional Chinese medicine, cherries are advised to treat the stomach, the spleen, and the blood. Cherries are believed to have a warming quality and can help to treat arthritis and rheumatism. The fruit is known to contain generous doses of vitamin C, iodine, and antioxidants, which makes it highly anti-inflammatory.

Maple

Maple is a fast-growing tree that brightens up the autumn landscape with its mesmerizing red and golden leaves. It also has beautiful winged seeds that spiral through the wind and create wondrous spectacles as they float away from their mother tree.

In many ancient cultures, maple was regarded as the Tree of

Light. Saulteaux, the creator god of the aboriginal Canadians, lived in a maple grove and taught the locals how to collect the sweet maple sap without harming the trees. The sugar maple's sap is used for making maple sirup, which is a long tradition in Canada where maple became the national tree. Because of its connection to Saulteaux, the warm light of the autumn maple leaves legendarily repels darkness and evil.

The Chippewa people called the maple spirit Mishosha and believed that he evolved from an evil wizard into a kind, compassionate one who helped others. That's why the tree has been regarded as a tree of balance between the light and dark parts of a soul. Maple inspires inner harmony. Its wisdom teaches us how to take in and exude light but also where to cast shadows if needed without letting the darkness overpower us. With the maple's help we may learn that our shadow could actually support our light if we can tame and understand it.

Since maple wood is excellent for sound transmission, it is used for making musical instruments. That's why it has also been linked to the magic of music and musical expression.

In natural medicine, maple was considered holy by various Native American peoples. They used its leaves in natural medicine as a general purifier, but mainly to treat sores, coughs, and gynecological issues. Maple leaves are lightly sedative, which makes them an excellent calming remedy. Maple infusion is also advised for cleansing the liver.

Walnut

Walnut is a slow-growing but hardy tree that may reach generous heights and live for many hundreds of years. In ancient Mesopotamia, walnuts were held in high esteem and grew in the legendary Hanging Gardens of Babylon. In ancient Greece, walnuts were sought for their wisdom and power of prophecy. The Old Greek name for walnuts, *caryon*, relates to the word *cara* that translates both to "head" and "tree crown." The Latin word for walnut is *jūglans*, which comes from the name *Jōvis glans* that translates to "the nut of Jupiter." Because of this, walnut has been regarded a tree of abundance not only on a physical but also on a spiritual level.

The walnut resembles the brain, and for this reason, both the tree and its fruit were considered to have a good effect on brain function. In magic, walnuts awaken us to our prophetic gifts and harmonize our conscious and subconscious minds. Furthermore, the nuts are very nutritious and contain high amounts of protein, vitamin E, and omega-3 fatty acids. They are known to be immune boosting and are even believed to cleanse the bloodstream. One has to be careful when picking walnuts, though, as the husks have a strong colorant, which has actually been used for dying fabrics and hair.

Walnut leaves have a special, sweet smell, and inhaling it helps us connect with the powerful walnut spirit. Resting under a walnut's crown provides clarity, inspiration, and insight. It's a tree of thinkers, philosophers, and sages.

Chestnut

Along with oak and beech, the chestnut comes from the Fagaceae tree family of exceptionally hardy, long-living, and majestic trees. There are two main kinds of chestnut trees: horse chestnut and sweet chestnut.

The horse chestnut can be recognized by its cone-shaped flower clusters and smooth, brown nuts, which are actually deadly poisonous to humans and must not be consumed. Nevertheless, everyone may feel pulled to pick up the nut when they see it lying on the ground as it's so beautifully smooth and shiny. In fact, carrying these nuts in one's pocket is believed to bring good fortune. In pagan tradition, keeping a chestnut as a talisman ensured good health, strength, and vitality. The nuts were also believed to protect us from negative entities. Placing chestnuts under your pillow at night creates a powerful shield around you and brings about beautiful, even prophetic, dreams.

The sweet chestnut tree has, as opposed to the horse chestnut, edible nuts that are very nutritious but should only be consumed roasted. The husks are spikier than those of the horse chestnut, which gives them an even more powerful guardian-type energy. The ancient Greeks loved the sweet chestnut tree, and a town called Kastanies has been named after the local name for this tree, *castanea*.

Along with the walnut tree, the sweet chestnut was regarded as the tree of god Zeus (Roman Jupiter). This made the nuts the perfect token for attracting financial stability as well as spiritual fulfillment. Curiously, sweet chestnut is a tree species that was not demonized during medieval Catholic Christianization and was actually believed to symbolize purity.

Almond

The almond tree loves heat and therefore grows only in warm climates. Since it's the first tree to bloom in the Mediterranean springtime, it has been known as the tree of renewal and new beginnings. Almond has a feminine presence, and its ancient name *amygdala* relates to the Sumerian words *ama ga*, which translate as "great mother."

The tree has also been linked to the ancient Phrygian goddess Kybele or Cybele, the mother of the gods. Cybele arose from a hermaphrodite called Agdistis after it was castrated by the gods. From the blood that spilled on the soil after the separation of the male and female reproductive organs sprouted two trees: an almond and a pomegranate. Cybele was a goddess of nature, fertility, healing, and time. Her power animal was a lion, and she can actually be seen in the Tarot card Strength as the woman who gently tames a lion. Cybele's later counterpart seems to be the Greek mother goddess Rhea who was also depicted with lions.

The almond is an important tree in Jewish mysticism. In ancient Israel, the almond tree was seen as the Tree of Life. The staffs of both Moses and Aaron were made from almond, and the two patriarchs performed various miracles with them. Moreover, almond is important in symbolism. In sacred geometry, the ancient teaching that applies philosophical meaning to geometry, it represents the mandorla which means "almond" in Italian. This powerful symbol has been seen as the gateway into other realities and as the mother goddess because its shape resembles the vulva. It also represents the third eye and our ability to see beyond the veil of time and space.

Almond nuts are consumed for their high levels of protein, calcium, magnesium, vitamin E, and omega-3 fatty acids. Ayurvedic medicine recommends a handful of almonds as a daily treat to strengthen the body's immunity. However, it's important to note that there's also a poisonous kind of almond (*Prunus dulcis amara*), which has broader but smaller nuts with a strikingly bitter taste.

In magic, the almond tree connects us with the divine feminine and through it lets us better understand its polarity – the divine masculine. Its nuts may even help us explore our inner sight and the ability to see otherworldly beings and realms. Furthermore, the almond blesses new beginnings and renewal in general.

Olive

The olive is a leafy, evergreen tree that thrives in subtropical climates. It's a very hardy tree, and some of the oldest olives are believed to be thousands of years old. Its wrinkled trunk creates wondrous, gnarled shapes, and its crown emits a soft, ethereal light because its leaves are dark green on top and pale, almost white, beneath.

The olive has a strong position in mythology and magic, especially in ancient Greece where it was considered a holy tree. The sacred olive trees of Athens were called *moria* and were venerated as the divine heritage from gods to men. The olive tree also became a Greek symbol of peace, justice, and deep wisdom. A mighty olive tree grew on the Acropolis next to the temple of goddess Athena who had an olive tree as one of her strongest attributes.

The fruit from this tree was used to fuel a sacred golden lamp that stood beside it and burned all year long. When the stronghold of Athens was burned down during the Persian invasion, the fire could not kill the mother olive tree as it revived the next day and continued to thrive for six hundred years. Therefore, the olive was probably one of the Trees of Light mentioned in chapter one. Even today, olive oil is used as fuel in the Jewish menorah, the seven-branched candlestick.

In ancient Morocco, the olive tree was the World Tree of Life, the column of the world. Furthermore, its leaves were believed to have sacred letters and words written on them, and the group spirit of the olive species was considered a wise prophet.

In Christian art, the olive was a symbol of renewal. In the tale of Noah and the Ark, a dove with an olive leaf in its beak came as the herald of a new land that rose from the seas after the deluge. In magic, the olive is the tree of enlightenment by which we may receive wisdom and inspiration. Olive fruit and leaves have been used in money spells. As tokens, they attract vitality, spiritual insights, and abundance.

Olive blossom is very fragrant, and the fruit has been used as food and medicine since ancient times. The fruit is either pickled or processed into olive oil, which is considered one of the healthiest oils there is. The fruit is high in antioxidants and vitamin E, and it helps maintain a healthy digestive system. It's also beneficial for brain function and helps improve memory.

The olive leaf is antibacterial and antifungal and has therefore been used in natural medicine to support the immune system and reduce inflammation.

Sycamore (Fig Tree)

Sycamore, also known as the fig tree, reaches great heights and widths. The fascinating fact about sycamore is that in the Mediterranean, it flowers and bears fruit almost the whole year long but mainly between the summer and winter solstices.

The ancient Egyptians held the sycamore in high esteem as it was linked to many important goddesses such the creator goddess Neith, the protectress of the dead Selket, and the sky goddesses Nuit and Hathor. Locals nourished sycamores with fresh water from the River Nile and made offerings such as fruit in order to keep the goddesses content. Moreover, the ancient Egyptians believed that during the soul's journey through the afterlife, a holy sycamore was reached after the dangers of the netherworld had been passed and, from its crown, sycamore goddesses offered the soul fruit and the water of life before the final passage to eternal life.

The sycamore tree is also of great importance in Buddhism as it was the Bodhi or Bo Tree, also called the Tree of Awakening, beneath which Siddhartha Gautama found *bodhi*, meaning enlightenment, and thus became a Buddha. The biblical Tree of Knowledge of Good and Evil that Eve and Adam ate from was originally a fig tree, and although it was replaced with apple over time, in most ancient depictions the couple is shown hiding their private parts with fig leaves. The sycamore is also an important tree in Roman mythology. A wild sycamore tree called Ficus Ruminalis was believed to grow near the banks of the Tiber where Romulus and Remus were nurtured by the motherly she-wolf. Furthermore, next to that sacred sycamore stood the temple of Diva Rumina, a goddess of birth and babies.

Figs bear highly nutritious fruit that is a good source of minerals such as iron, magnesium, calcium, and potassium. In magic, the sycamore is a tree of enlightenment and spiritual awakening. For this reason, it's a wonderful journey tree as it offers insights into the afterlife and the dimensions that co-exist with ours in the World Tree of Life. Moreover, its feminine group spirit was believed to help women conceive and is often asked to bless babies in magical spells.

Rose Hip

The rose hip is a wild shrub that likes to grow in hedgerows where it can imbibe plenty of sunshine. One of the most common rose hip species is called the dog rose (*Rosa canina*). It's a hardy, climbing shrub with thorny branches that produce vitamin-rich fruit. Dogs as well as the rose hip spirits have been known as beings of unconditional love. That's why these beautiful shrubs were adored by the Greek goddess of love, Aphrodite, who is believed to often manifest in their vicinity.

Later, in Christianity, the rose became a symbol of the Virgin Mary and inspired the name of the prayer psalter, the rosary, and the string of beads that is used to count the rosary prayers. The rose is also at the center of the Calvary cross that symbolizes the Rosicrucian movement, which originated in the 17th century and spread the wisdom of the ancient esoteric traditions such as Hermeticism or spiritual alchemy.

In natural magic, rose hip is considered a highly protective shrub. Thanks to its thorny armor that repels harsh energies, the rose hip invites only love and beauty. Its warm and guardian-type energy inspires us to balance our gentle, empathetic self with our spirit warrior that stands up for us in times of need. Moreover, its five-petaled blossom relates to a pagan symbol of psychic protection, the pentagram, which only fortifies its shielding quality.

Rose hip fruit usually ripens at the end of September and is used in natural medicine thanks to its high levels of vitamin C, beta-carotene, flavonoids, and antioxidants. The fascinating fact is that the vitamins are preserved even after boiling, which makes rose hip tea a perfect drink for the winter months.

In magic, rose hip makes a powerful companion for banishing and shielding rituals as well as love spells. It also helps us with romantic love, though it usually guides us to start with ourselves first, therefore inspiring us to learn more about self-love and self-appreciation. Rose hip fruit can be carried or kept by the bedside to help us attract affection and romance, but also to provide psychic protection

INDEX

alchemical, 99, 123, 195

alder, 50, 121, 174, 175

almond, 17, 66, 199, 200

ancient Egypt, 13, 56

ancient Greece, 22, 44, 76, 197, 200

ancient Rome, 22

Anglo-Saxon, 110, 125, 166, 193

ankh, 58, 60

Apollo, 44, 78, 173

apple, 22, 23, 44, 48, 65, 122, 162, 163, 202

ash, 46, 50, 65, 121, 123, 146, 159, 171, 178, 179, 180, 187

aspen, 124, 182, 183, 184

Avalon, 48, 122, 162

Axis Mundi, 3, 27

Bacchus, 60, 176, 189

Baikal, 21, 37, 41

Baltic, 19, 51, 74, 170

Bennu bird, 57

Bible, 16, 66, 79, 163

birch, 21, 37, 121, 128, 146, 157, 158, 172, 182

bird, 3, 36, 41, 44, 56, 57, 61, 70, 73, 78, 79, 80, 99, 109, 114, 150, 151, 152, 153, 163, 169, 187

blackthorn, 123, 185, 186

Bodhi Tree, 10, 39, 115

Brigid, 36, 65, 67, 75, 117, 158

broom, 123, 158, 190

Buddha, 10, 11, 39, 40, 49, 50, 83, 115, 176, 202

Celtic, 22, 23, 24, 29, 34, 36, 48, 49, 50, 51, 63, 66, 70, 75, 77, 110, 112, 117, 120, 158, 161, 162, 164, 169, 170, 172, 175, 178, 180

Celts, 23, 63, 119, 120, 164, 166, 169, 172, 173, 175, 176, 181, 183, 184

Cernunnos, 48, 50, 70

Channel, 3, 27, 31, 32, 33, 34, 42, 79, 87, 110, 115, 124, 131, 139

Cherry, 195

chestnut, 198

Chinese, 42, 74, 195

Christian mysticism, 31

Christianization, 50, 66, 76, 93, 131, 165, 171, 181, 198

Conifers, 88, 175

Cosmic Tree, 11, 12, 13, 17, 20, 22, 25

cycles, 20, 23, 44, 51, 83, 84, 85, 86, 87, 88, 89, 90, 91, 92, 94, 114, 116, 120, 121, 123, 127, 128, 138, 185

Czech, 32, 48, 50, 51, 151, 160, 179, 195

devas, 40, 46, 47, 50, 51, 52, 188

dimensions, 24, 27, 29, 36, 55, 59, 73, 78, 87, 104, 112, 113, 115, 122, 124, 129, 134, 139, 151, 203

Dionysus, 60, 176, 189

distaff, 64, 65, 66, 67, 83, 113, 120

divination, 63, 118, 121, 122, 126, 128, 159, 181

djed, 13, 58, 59, 60

DNA, 53, 80, 123, 147, 189

double helix, 53, 80, 103, 189

Druid, 170, 180

Druidic, 3, 157, 169, 177

Druids, 24, 117, 118, 119, 120, 131, 139, 140, 170, 173, 186, 188

Egyptian, 12, 24, 40, 46, 47, 56, 57, 58, 60, 67, 70, 76, 77, 78, 109, 176

elder, 50, 123, 164, 165, 182

electromagnetic field, 28, 29, 31, 32, 33, 34, 36, 55, 57, 80, 84, 87, 97, 98, 99, 100, 102,

103, 104, 106, 110, 113, 114, 115, 150, 152, 178

elements, 19, 29, 47, 76, 113, 122, 128, 137, 138, 139, 153, 157, 159, 173

elf, 121, 175

elm, 48, 50, 123, 164, 180, 181, 182, 183

Fates, 33, 52, 64, 83, 84, 113, 180

Faunus, 22, 46, 51

fig, 13, 46, 202

fir, 123

Flower of Life, 100, 103, 109

Garden of the Hesperides, 22, 163

Germanic, 18, 19, 20, 32, 48, 50, 51, 63, 109, 110, 117, 170, 175, 193

gorse, 123, 186, 187

Greek, 22, 23, 24, 42, 44, 46, 47, 50, 57, 60, 65, 70, 76, 77, 78, 109, 163, 164, 166, 170, 172, 176, 179, 180, 189, 197, 199, 200, 203

Green Man, 50, 93, 122, 170, 171

Hathor, 40, 77, 202

hawthorn, 122, 184, 185, 186

hazel, 63, 122, 162, 172, 173, 174

heather, 124, 187, 191

Hermes, 42, 44, 70, 78, 99, 122, 124, 173, 174, 180, 182

holly, 122, 171, 172

Icelandic, 34, 125

Inanna, 41, 70, 78

Incas, 25, 47

interdimensional, 9, 31, 32, 33, 34, 55, 56, 80, 98, 129, 150, 162, 165, 179, 190

Ireland, 48, 110, 117, 119, 173

Irminsul, 19, 31, 37, 128, 142

Isis, 13, 70, 78

ivy, 123, 188, 189

Jesus Christ, 16, 66, 67, 87

journey, 17, 27, 28, 31, 34, 83, 86, 88, 91, 127, 133, 135, 136, 137, 140, 145, 147, 148, 149, 151, 152, 161, 182, 202, 203, 211

journeying, 31, 33, 110, 122, 134, 139, 147, 149, 150, 164, 174

Kabbalistic, 14, 17

kundalini, 13, 28, 79, 99, 115, 150, 189

ladder, 21, 27, 31, 55

light body, 27, 29, 55, 95, 98, 100, 104, 106, 113, 115, 128

Lilith, 41, 163

linden, 5, 51, 147, 193, 194, 211

maple, 146, 195, 196

meditation, 33, 110, 127, 129, 136, 141, 164

Mercury, 70, 99, 122, 124, 173, 174, 180, 182

Merkaba, 29, 100, 106, 110, 128, 211

Merlin, 23, 49, 121, 176

Mesopotamia, 13, 41, 42, 56, 163, 197

Mesopotamian, 19, 41, 42, 47, 48, 56, 60, 70, 78, 176

Milky Way, 11, 19, 36, 185

Moses, 14, 16, 66, 70, 199

Mystics, 17, 28, 86, 109, 157, 174

Native American, 25, 176, 183, 196

Norns, 19, 33, 36, 52, 64, 65, 84, 113, 120, 125, 180

Norse, 11, 18, 20, 31, 32, 34, 36, 46, 50, 56, 63, 65, 76, 79, 88, 109, 110, 113, 117, 120, 124, 125, 137, 158, 164, 173, 178, 179, 182, 191, 193

nymphs, 22, 46, 47, 52, 164, 180, 182, 193

oak, 24, 44, 46, 48, 51, 67, 122, 166, 169, 170, 171, 172, 191, 193, 198

Odin, 19, 34, 49, 50, 63, 79, 98, 117, 124, 125, 128, 173, 176, 179

ogham, 23, 24, 117, 118, 119, 120, 121, 123, 125, 129, 130, 133, 136, 165, 172, 180, 181, 183, 187, 188, 189, 190, 191

olive, 13, 44, 65, 135, 146, 180, 200, 201

Osiris, 12, 13, 46, 57, 70, 176

Our Tree of Life, 29, 98, 102, 126, 139

Paleolithic, 24, 109

Pan, 22, 46, 51, 176

pillar, 13, 19, 21, 31, 44, 58, 60, 99

pine, 46, 60, 64, 175, 176, 191

pinecone, 60, 70, 189

pole, 16, 21, 25, 27, 31, 55, 93, 122, 171, 172

portals, 28, 34, 52

psychopomp, 44, 79, 171

Ptah, 57, 60

Q'ero, 25, 47

reed, 123, 190

Roman, 44, 46, 50, 51, 61, 63, 70, 170, 172, 173, 182, 189, 198, 202

rose hip, 203, 204

rowan, 50, 121, 158, 159, 162

runes, 37, 50, 63, 64, 65, 109, 110, 117, 120, 125, 127, 129, 130, 132, 133, 136, 141, 173, 211

Saxons, 19, 31, 179

serpent, 3, 16, 17, 19, 36, 40, 41, 42, 44, 48, 57, 61, 63, 64, 65, 70, 73, 74, 76, 77, 78, 79, 80, 99, 110, 114, 117, 123, 134, 150, 151, 152, 153, 163, 189

serpentine, 16, 19, 22, 42, 73, 74, 77, 134, 150, 151, 188, 189

shamanic, 21, 24, 32, 33, 49, 55, 63, 77, 80, 98, 125, 127, 128, 148, 161, 179

shamanic journey, 49, 63, 98, 125

shamanism, 55, 56, 194

shield, 131, 134, 153, 198

Siberia, 21, 22

Siddhartha, 39, 74, 202

Sidhe, 34, 122, 123, 124, 163, 181

Slavs, 20, 48, 51, 75, 193

spindle, 33, 83

spinning, 52, 65, 83, 84, 113, 158

Sun Wheel, 14, 20

swan, 21, 36, 37, 75, 79, 109, 117, 129, 150

sycamore, 13, 40, 202, 203

symbols, 9, 14, 21, 33, 37, 48, 51, 58, 64, 65, 77, 95, 100, 109, 110, 112, 115, 117, 122, 125, 127, 129, 132, 133, 136, 149, 170, 190

third eye, 19, 35, 60, 91, 121, 123, 161, 162, 174, 176, 189, 199

thyrsus, 60, 189

toroidal, 29, 32, 84, 87, 100, 102, 106, 152

torus, 29, 31, 32, 33, 55, 57, 80, 84, 87, 98, 99, 100, 104, 106, 110, 114, 115, 124, 178

Tree of Life, 3, 7, 9, 10, 11, 12, 13, 14, 16, 17, 19, 21, 22, 23, 25, 27, 28, 29, 31, 32, 33, 36, 37, 41, 42, 44, 47, 48, 49, 51, 52, 53, 55, 56, 57, 61, 64, 65, 70, 73, 76, 77, 78, 80, 84, 87, 88, 94, 95, 97, 98, 99, 100, 102, 104, 106, 107, 109, 110, 112, 113, 114, 115, 117, 119, 122, 124, 125, 128, 129, 131, 132, 133, 134, 139, 141, 142, 149, 150, 151, 152, 153, 158, 169, 170, 176, 178, 179, 181, 188, 199, 201, 203

Tree of Light, 14, 196

vine, 50, 122, 123, 164, 182, 189

vortex, 29, 31, 32, 33, 34, 55, 80, 87, 98, 99, 100, 102, 106, 115

walnut, 46, 135, 197, 198

wand, 64, 132, 134, 139, 148, 159

was-scepter, 56, 57, 58, 60, 67

white poplar, 124, 183, 184

willow, 41, 44, 46, 121, 160, 161, 179

World Pillar, 27, 37, 59, 128, 142

World Tree, 3, 7, 9, 13, 18, 19, 25, 27, 28, 29, 31, 32, 33, 34, 36, 37, 41, 42, 44, 47, 48, 49, 50, 51, 52, 53, 55, 56, 61, 63, 64, 65, 70, 73, 76, 77, 78, 79, 80, 84, 87, 88, 94, 95, 98, 99, 100, 102, 104, 106, 107, 109, 110, 112, 113, 114, 115, 117, 119, 122, 124, 125, 128, 129, 131, 132, 133, 139, 141, 142, 150, 151, 152, 170, 178, 179, 188, 201, 203

World Tree of Life, 9, 27, 28, 44, 51, 65, 73, 87, 126, 139, 142

yew, 32, 48, 64, 88, 124, 129, 169, 177, 178, 179

Yggdrasil, 18, 19, 34, 50, 65, 79, 113, 125

yoga, 13, 79, 99

ABOUT THE AUTHOR

Iva Kenaz is an award-winning author from Prague, Bohemia, whose books are significantly influenced by metaphysics and natural magic. She studied Screenwriting at the Prague Film Academy and holds an MA in Creative Writing. She's also an avid researcher of ancient knowledge and a practitioner of runes, tarot, and green magic.

Iva's many visionary books include *The Witch Within, The Goddess Within, The Merkaba Mystery, Alchemist Awakening: An Alchemical Journey Through the Zodiac, Manifested, Francois Villon, Sacred Geometry and Magical Symbols, Runes: Magical Codes of Nature,* and *Tree Magic: The Path of Druids, Shamans, and Mystics.*

The author, Iva Kenaz, with one of her linden staffs.

Printed in Dunstable, United Kingdom